TESTIMONIALS

"It is rare to find someone that will challenge you to be your best self! However, this is exactly what Dominick does. His vision of the field, what is needed for fulfillment, and ability to take your performance to the next level is extraordinary. If you are wondering what is next for you, how to use the gifts that are in you, and how you can make a greater impact on the world then this book may be your answer!"

STEVE WILT
SVP FINANCIAL ADVISOR, CAPTRUST

"This book will elevate your leadership no matter where you are in your life journey. I recently left my comfort zone in a corporate environment after 31 years. I am absolutely energized and excited about living into my second chapter. I've leveraged many of the tools and lessons you'll read about in this book to launch my new venture from a place of deep purpose. Because of that, I feel a sense of meaning and excitement every day. Read thoughtfully, and take action accordingly!"

MICHAEL YOUNG
CONSULTANT & EXECUTIVE COACH

"Dominick has an incredible talent for peeling back the layers to uncover what is holding people back from their true potential. In this book, Dominick shares inspiring stories of how he's guided his clients to find purpose, clarity and insight in both their personal and professional lives, which is what he's brought to my life. Working with Dominick is like having someone see into your soul. He has helped me change my life for the better, and by reading this book, you will too."

TINA SCHACKMAN
BENEFIT FINANCIAL SERVICES GROUP
PRINCIPAL, SR. RETIREMENT PLAN CONSULTANT

"I had the privilege of attending Dominick's Design Your Next Decade women's retreat for high performing women in male dominated industries. We embarked upon a journey - as you will by reading this book - to bring out our desires, passions and focus in life. By tapping into my purpose, I found the confidence to create an intentional and energizing path forward, which I'm living today. In that same way, this book will challenge you to make bold decisions and lead with confidence so you can inspire others to make the changes they want in their lives."

MINDY O'CONNOR
ASCENSUS, HEAD OF BUSINESS DEVELOPMENT

"Dominick is like an angel. After building a successful investment management practice, completing 5 Ironmans, then adding two young kids to the mix later in life, I lost my footing. Dominick came into my life during a time of desperate need to care for my health and my mind after burnout landed me in the back of an ambulance with a panic attack. In this book, he shares with you many of the life changing tools and methods of self discovery he taught me to reconnect with purpose and take back life on my terms. The same potential awaits you by reading this book."

TERI KELLEY
SVP MORGAN STANLEY

*"By his mere presence one
who has reformed himself
is able to reform thousands,
though he may not utter
a single word."*

PARAMAHANSA YOGANANDA

Master the Art
of Leading Yourself to
Inspire and Impact Others

ON PURPOSE LEADERSHIP

DOMINICK QUARTUCCIO

978-19-5-036757-3

Published in 2020

ISBN: 978-19-5-036757-3

Editing and publishing by Kelly Irving
kellyirving.com

Cover design and internal layout by Ellie Schroeder
ellieschroeder.com

dominickq.com

To all of my clients who have chosen the path less traveled.

You are doing the inner work, living your best self, and inspiring others to do the same.

Thank you for blazing the trail and leaving a path for others to follow.

CONTENTS

ABOUT THE AUTHOR

Dominick Quartuccio's passion is helping people become the best versions of themselves.

As an international speaker, author, and executive coach for high-performing leaders in pressure-rich environments, he helps successful and incredibly busy professionals connect to their purpose, communicate bold visions, and lead meaningful change.

Dominick is on the forefront of leading men who are doing inner work – becoming better leaders, partners, and fathers. He co-hosts *The Great Man Within* podcast and runs The Great Man Mastermind, a community of high-caliber and high-character men living their greatest purpose.

He is also an outspoken advocate of and champion for women doing inner work. He's a regular speaker on the stages of women's events, such as TEDx Wilmington Women, One More Woman, and Women in Pensions network. He also runs the Design Your Future women's retreat, supporting women in male-dominated businesses to design futures they can't wait to live into.

This is Dominick's second book. His first, *Design Your Future: 3 Simple Steps to Stop Drifting and Take Command of Your Life*, was published in 2017.

You might have heard Dominick on *NPR*, read about him in the *New York Times*, or watched him do 100 consecutive pushups on YouTube. (Serious, go look.)

But on most days, you can find Dominick meditating, drinking Bulletproof coffee, or devouring a good book.

dominickq.com

INTRODUCTION

"What you do speaks so loudly I cannot hear what you say."

- RALPH WALDO EMERSON

Whitney's stomach dropped.

She felt the acute sensation that accompanies feedback that's long overdue and laced with the uncomfortable truth.

"I say this because I care about you, Whitney. The very behaviors you said you want to change in your team, you just embodied yourself, reinforcing the status quo in front of all of them."

I delivered this difficult message to Whitney 24 hours after her first team offsite with her top 50 leaders.

A few months earlier, Whitney had been given a big promotion.

She was appointed the division head of a Fortune 100 organization, a business where she'd spent her entire 25-year career.

I'd known Whitney for years. She was talented, smart, and a universally respected leader in her company. She was put in charge of an essential part of a mature business that desperately needed an infusion of bold, forward-thinking leadership. She was perfect.

Whitney could see capable leaders who'd become too comfortable managing the existing state of the business at the expense of leading into the future.

The culture in her business had become conservative, complacent, and averse to the discomfort that comes with making meaningful change.

Whitney knew she needed to shake up the system.

I knew they'd picked the right person to lead that charge.

Whitney contacted me about delivering a kick-off keynote speech for her first company offsite.

This offsite would be Whitney's first time bringing her top 50 leaders together, a team who oversaw an organization of roughly 1,500 associates.

Whitney wanted to signal in the dawn of a new day by blowing off the doors of what her leaders had come to expect from traditional offsite experiences.

"I want every person to leave this offsite feeling like that was the best 24 hours they've ever spent at a business meeting," she briefed me in. "It will be unmistakable that this is not business as usual. They will be 100-percent clear that we are going to lead differently from this point forward."

I was inspired by Whitney's vision, so I agreed to do the speech.

When the day arrived, Whitney was the first speaker scheduled to take the stage. It was her big moment to set the tone and communicate her vision. I was scheduled to follow her and hammer the message home.

I settled myself in the back row among the 50 leaders as Whitney took the stage.

Leaning forward in my seat, I was ready to feel the full force of Whitney's new charge to her leaders.

But...

It never came.

Whitney delivered 20 minutes of eloquent, professional speech that was certainly becoming of a division leader.

But she was not bold.

She was conservative.
She was safe.
She was *status quo.*

Whitney delivered a speech that I have heard hundreds of times before in corporate settings.

She referred to *"the need to change"* and the *"need to act with urgency,"* but nothing *felt* different.

100 TIMES BEFORE

Looking around at her 50 leaders, it was painfully obvious they felt the same way. I watched many of them switching their attention between Whitney on stage and the devices in their hands.

They'd sat through countless other presentations with leaders saying the same thing.

As a result, Whitney failed to inspire her leaders the way she'd hoped. They left that offsite feeling the same way as every other day at the office.

The following day, I sat down with Whitney to have an uncomfortable conversation about what I'd experienced.

"You cannot ask your leaders to be bold and face the discomfort that comes with change unless you're willing to embody that yourself," I explained.

"You didn't do that yesterday. You defaulted to your typical communication style, which is polished, eloquent, and safe. That's not what your people needed."

I said my piece
with love, care, and
compassion.

"The very behaviors you said you want to change in your team, you just embodied yourself...reinforcing the status quo...in front of all of them. They need to see you being bold. They need to see you stepping towards discomfort, modeling urgency and living the change. *You need to show them the way.*"

The color drained from Whitney's face. (She takes extraordinary pride in her leadership, so she felt like she'd let her people down. Even worse, she'd let herself down. I'm sure you can relate.)

"You're right," she said, restoring her posture with a newfound sense of determination. "I can see why leading others to change their behaviors is so difficult. Hell, I didn't even realize how resistant I was to change until just now. I need to be the example if I want to have any hope of leading others to this new vision I've laid out. *What do I need to do to become the leader my people need me to be?*"

With that shift, Whitney made the most important decision any leader can make:

A commitment to master the art of leading herself first so that she can then inspire and impact others.

2

THE TWO PROBLEMS OF TODAY'S LEADERSHIP

Whitney's story is all too common.

As someone who has worked with hundreds of leaders and teams, in both business and personal environments, I see two connected problems in how leaders, like Whitney, are leading today.

1

PROBLEM #1:

Leaders are trying to lead others before mastering the art of leading themselves.

Leaders always ask me the same three questions:

1 How do I get my people to change?

2 How do I get my people to act with more urgency?

3 How do I hold my people accountable?

If you've paid close enough attention, you'll realize there's a fatal flaw in all of these questions:

They assume the answers lie within the followers, not the leader.

There are legions of leaders today running around and pointing the finger at everyone else but themselves when it comes to leading change, doing what's uncomfortable and executing on the most important priorities.

There are a select few who point those fingers at themselves first.

These are what I call *On Purpose Leaders.*

On Purpose Leaders know their "why," make every decision with intentionality, and live the example they wish to inspire in others.

» Instead of asking, "How do I get my people to change?" they ask, "How do I change?"

» Instead of asking, "How do I get my people to ask with urgency?" they ask, "How do I act with urgency?"

» Instead of asking, "How do I hold my people accountable?" they ask, "How will I hold myself accountable?"

Too many leaders have not yet mastered the art of leading themselves, yet they expect to be masterful leaders of others.

It simply doesn't work this way.

Every inconsistency, blind spot, gap in integrity, and substandard behavior you have in leading yourself will be amplified in the levels beneath you.

This will be showcased in your teams' behaviors and results.

You must master the art of leading yourself before you can effectively lead others.

2

PROBLEM #2:

You cannot master the art of leading yourself without connecting to your purpose, and you cannot see your work as the enemy to purpose.

Executives, entrepreneurs, and community leaders constantly speak to me about their growing desire to find a deeper sense of purpose in their lives.

They want more than just a career and a paycheck.

They are seeking meaning, fulfillment, and aliveness.

Don't you?

But perhaps you've been sold a story that you're only truly free to pursue purpose once you're financially independent. Either that or you must disrupt an unreasonable amount of your life for work that pays little or far less than what you earn presently.

Many of the people I speak to believe purpose is some unattainable fantasy that exists in a parallel universe or must be a massive undertaking that'll take years or decades to realize.

They see their present-day work as the enemy; a necessary evil to meet mortgages, accelerate careers, and support families.

They'd really rather be doing something else.

Again, how about you?

If you're disconnected from a sense of purpose, then an essential part of your life force is left untapped!

You are leading with only a fraction of your potential.

Your teams will feel it.

Your results will reflect it.

You cannot master the art of leading yourself without connecting to your purpose.

You must see your present-day work as a portal to your purpose, right here and now, in order for you to lead from your highest potential.

WHY IT'S IMPORTANT YOU ACT, NOW!

To explain why these two problems are such an issue, and why you must do something to change right now, let me tell you another story.

For the first 15 years of my career, I led sales teams in the high-pressure world of financial services for Prudential, a Fortune 100 firm. After leaving the industry to start my own consulting business, I've made a big part of my living coaching, speaking to, and training the financial services industry.

Over these last two decades, I've witnessed tremendous change ripple through an industry that was predicated on – and quite frankly, addicted to – stability.

There's been a dramatic shift in industry regulations, which has led to margin compression, rapid consolidation, and mass layoffs. This has resulted in much more work on the backs of far fewer people.

Before that shift, this was an industry where people spent their entire 30-, 40- and even 50-year careers without much dramatic change. Movements were incremental. Managing what already existed – which was often multiple billions of annual revenue – was valued over leading change, which could often bring risk and disruption.

All of a sudden, the industry found its financials shifting rapidly, but its people were still largely clinging to the old promise of stability, familiarity, and "what's always worked before."

All of a sudden, lifelong "managers" were being asked to lead change in organizations filled with people who'd been raised in a culture of preserving the status quo.[1]

---

1 I define managers as those whose job is to protect what currently exists versus leading people into new frontiers of behavior, business, and ways of being.

These managers would say all the right things, but their teams wouldn't respond because the manager wouldn't be modeling the behavior he or she spoke of.

These managers would then get frustrated at the lack of movement in their teams, pointing the finger at their people for being unwilling to change or not acting with enough urgency.

That's when I noticed a troubling theme emerge: *These managers were embodying the very behavior they wished to change in their people.*

Like Whitney from the opening story, they themselves still had deeply rooted desires for comfort, stability, and sticking with what's always worked for them.

They welcomed change, as long as it was incremental and felt safe.

But their businesses demanded transformational change.

This isn't just relegated to financial services. Every industry is under tremendous pressure to adapt, grow, and speed up in accordance with our technologically hyper-charged and ever-changing world.

There's a second big theme that's emerged as I've worked alongside leaders of all businesses:

More and more people are seeking a deeper sense of purpose in their lives and view the all-encompassing demands of their work to be the barrier to meaning and fulfillment.

People are working longer hours, always connected to their devices and with a relentless emphasis on nonstop productivity.

That never-ending,
intense pressure
is causing people to ask:
"Is this worth it?"

As people are grinding their ways to better business results at the expense of their health, relationships, and personal freedoms, the need for a deeper sense of purpose becomes increasingly more crucial to staying fully engaged in their lives.

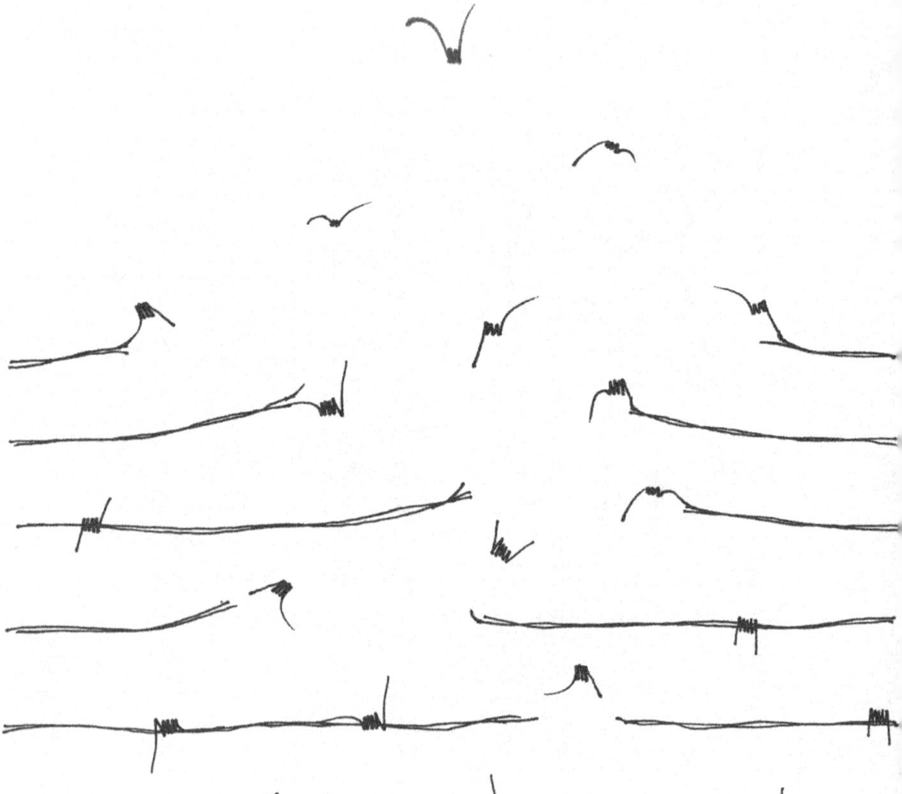

When I made the announcement to leave behind a wonderful 15-year career to pursue my dream, a colleague likened my exit to a prison break:

> It was like you made this sudden break for the fences, and as you sprinted across the prison yard and the dogs were in pursuit with the guards shooting at you...the rest of us were pounding on our bars and cheering you on from our jail cells...you jumped the face and you made it out!

While I found this scene amusing, conjuring up images from *Shawshank Redemption*, it also stirred up a subtle sadness.

A sadness that he, like so many others as I came to learn, felt on a deeper level that the never-ending demands of his work life felt like a not-so-subtle prison cell.

I don't want the people I care about to live their lives this way.

I don't want you to live your life this way.

The good news is, you don't have to.

I've worked with incredible leaders – like Whitney – who came to the awakening that all of the success of their leadership hinged upon looking inwards first.

When you connect to purpose and master the art of leading yourself, leading others becomes easier and more fulfilling.

Your mere presence will inspire others to raise their standards and meet you where you're at.

This book is your guide to leading On Purpose.

It requires you draw a line in the sand, right now, and step into a new way of leading.

Inside, you will discover the
four tenets of the On Purpose Leader:

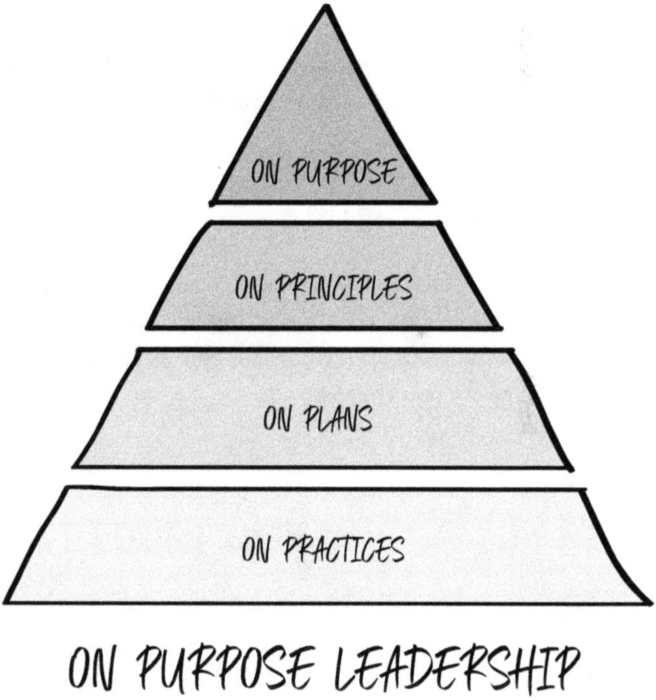

1

ON PURPOSE

Your purpose consists of knowing what gives you your greatest energy, leading with intentionality, and surrounding yourself with people who demand the highest version of you. **Your purpose leaves the world a better place than how you found it.**

2

ON PRINCIPLES

Your principles represent your beliefs and guide how you take action in accordance with living your purpose. **Your principles show you the way.**

3 ON PLANS

Your plan is about execution, your way of bringing essence into form. Your plan must be simple, clear, and energizing. Y**our plans make victory inevitable.**

4 ON PRACTICES

Your practices refine the skills you need to live as an On Purpose Leader. These are the intentional routines and habits you will use to optimize your days, weeks, and years. **Your practices sharpen your sword.**

The On Purpose Leader Manifesto on the following pages articulates the beliefs, responsibilities, and required actions of an On Purpose Leader.

YOUR ON PURPOSE LEADER MANIFESTO

I encourage to read this out loud, sign your name, and step into your power today.

YOUR ON PURPOSE LEADER MANIFESTO

My name is
(fill in your name)

I am an On Purpose Leader.

On Purpose Leaders create environments where we and those we care about can thrive.

We are ushering in a new regime of On Purpose Leadership:

> We reject the idea of suspending our dreams and postponing fulfillment until the backend of life.
>
> We reject delivering results at the expense of our own physical, mental, emotional, and spiritual wellbeing, and of those we lead.

> We reject the idea that living our purpose must require a dramatic and complete upheaval of our lives.
>
> We reject the idea that feelings and emotions are the enemy to performance.
>
> We reject the idea that leading requires absence of fear, knowing all the answers, and going at it alone.

Because we are swimming in an ocean of businesses, cultures, and leaders who consciously and unconsciously reinforce the deeply entrenched beliefs outlined above...

...we must be a force for change.

We must be bold enough to break the rules.

We must be determined to define our own.

We believe:

In order to effectively lead others, we must first learn how to lead ourselves.

Our work is a portal to purpose, meaning, and fulfillment right here and now.

We hold 100-percent responsibility for the results and sustained health of our teams (and ourselves).

Developing emotional fluency is the path to taking bold, decisive, and aligned action.

We are the ones who get to define what it means to "be an On Purpose Leader."

A leader cannot realize his/her fullest potential without a community of other On Purpose Leaders.

The world is counting on us.

We must find one another and carry out this mission together.

MY PURPOSE
Leaves This World a Better Place Than I Found It

My PRINCIPLES
Show Me the Way

MY PLAN
Makes Victory Inevitable

MY PRACTICE
Sharpens My Sword

I create environments where I and those I lead can thrive.

I AM ON PURPOSE

X ______________________________

CHAPTER 1

OFF PURPOSE

Patrick came to me in deep disappointment after he'd been passed over for the National Head of Sales opening at his Fortune 500 company. He'd made it to the final two candidates, but ultimately the business went with an older, more experienced external candidate.

Patrick was much younger than what the business was used to entrusting for positions of that magnitude, so historically speaking it would've been an edge for the company.

He was proud that he showed up as his best self during every step of the evaluation process.

When I asked him if he would've changed anything

about how he showed up during that process, he said confidently, "Not a thing."

So I said, "Then the reason you didn't get the job isn't because of how you showed up during the evaluation process; it's because of how you showed up over the last 15 years of your career."

(Gut punch, landed.)

There was a long period of silence.

Finally, he said, "You're right."

In that moment, Patrick turned into a client.

Shortly thereafter, we began our work.

Yet I quickly noticed a troubling trend. Every call and meeting that we'd scheduled, he showed up late. Not egregiously, but it was five minutes here, 10 minutes there, even when we'd agreed that we were going to start on time.

I've known Patrick for a while. He's as good as they get. He's honest, smart, and treats people with respect. He's a devoted husband and father. I cared for him.

So I owed him the truth,
which I explained in
four simple words:

"I don't trust you."

I explained that every time I honored my word and he broke his, there was a crack in our bond of trust.

"How can I count on someone who doesn't deliver on what he says he's going to, or at the very least is so casual about his commitments that I'm left to question the integrity of his conviction?"

He took the shot like a champ. "You're absolutely right," he said. "I don't know why, but sometimes I find myself cutting corners and giving myself a pass on it. I've gotten really good at delivering a B effort and packaging it up so everyone thinks it's an A."

"Maybe people see your effort on some level as an A," I told him, "but people are far more attuned to your micro-behaviors than you think. Many people can't consciously put their finger on it, but it's the small things like showing up late, letting commitments slip, or not really listening intently to someone that cause them to distrust you."

Add those up, and the cumulative effect over a long enough period of time spells out: ***We can't trust you for the big leadership job.***

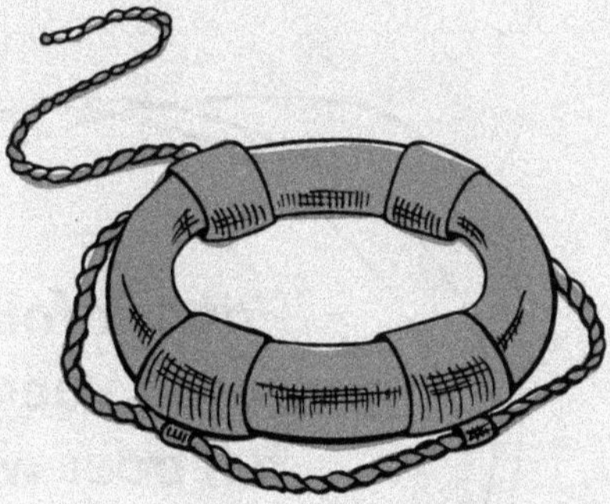

The light bulb went off for him.

He was drifting.

He'd been Off Purpose.

This intervention woke him up.

He could see all the ways he was cutting corners and showing up with a B+ effort when the situations called for excellence.

He could see how the long-term accumulation of those behaviors could erode just enough trust in his leadership that it kept him from getting the big job.

He absorbed the tough love and made an intentional declaration on the spot: "From this point forward, I'm a man you can trust."

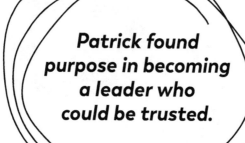

Patrick found purpose in becoming a leader who could be trusted.

He was never again late to one of our meetings.

He took this energy of intentionality back into the workplace.

He stopped cutting corners.

He stopped mailing in B+ efforts.

He led himself, On Purpose.

A year later, another big opportunity arose: the Chief Operating Officer position.

He'd never spent a day of his professional career in operations.

But it didn't matter.

This time, he got the job. He was promoted to the Chief Operating Officer role.

Shortly thereafter, his division was sold for $6 billion dollars, the single largest transaction in the history of his industry.

He was entrusted to lead that $6-billion-dollar transition.

That's the power of leading On Purpose.

DISTRUST: THE ONE REASON WHY THEY WILL RESIST YOUR LEADERSHIP

All resistance of your leadership can be boiled down to one thing: distrust.

As you just heard about in the case of Patrick, his two opportunities – the National Head of Sales and the Chief Operating Officer roles – hinged upon the organization's confidence in his ability to get the big job done.

Once he stopped drifting and showed up On Purpose, he landed the big job.

He had secured his company's trust.

3

Resistance of your leadership comes in three forms:

1. Distrust of *The System*
2. Distrust of *Themselves*
3. Distrust of *You*

While the effectiveness of your leadership will be impacted by each of those three reasons, the make-or-break is: distrust in *you.*

Distrust in you happens when you have not effectively mastered the art of leading yourself and are living off purpose.

I've seen excellent businesses (systems) and competent workers (themselves) reject the leadership of leaders they didn't trust.

Conversely, I've seen dysfunctional businesses, teams, and communities filled with people who doubt themselves yet have thrown their support behind a leader who inspires trust. A strong leader who commands trust can overcome organizational chaos and self-doubt from everyone.

So, the key to becoming an On Purpose Leader is to first understand how you are showing up in each of these areas of distrust.

#1 – Distrust of The System

You may be the most competent, capable, and qualified leader in the world, and yet you may still face blatant or covert resistance due to a deep-seeded distrust that your followers have in The System.

Some examples of The System include:

- » The government
- » Big business
- » The patriarchy
- » Organized religion
- » The institution of marriage
- » Authority figures

The people you lead are bringing a lifetime of experiences and deep-rooted conditioning to the present day (as are you).

Your people have been misled, betrayed, or at the very least disappointed by some of their life's experiences. They may attribute this pain and distrust to The System that wronged them. They are carrying this distrust with them everywhere they go, and it'll show up in your interactions with them.

» *"It doesn't matter how much I sell, they're going to double my sales goal again next year."*

» *"I can bust my ass and be the most qualified candidate, but the opportunity is going to go to ___________ (not me)."*

» *"This new initiative is the just the executive team's flavor of the month... I'll wait it out until the next new shiny thing they get excited about."*

All of these sentiments are both real and relevant to the person saying them AND a major drag on your ability to lead that person and the rest of your people forward.

I'm willing to bet you have your own distrust of certain systems.

Don't think so?

Let me place your fate in the hands of a call center or your local DMV and we'll see how trusting you are.

As an On Purpose Leader, you need to recognize that when systemic distrust pops up, it isn't about you.

It's about the system(s) that have failed your people in the past.

Many times, the people you lead will be unaware of this systemic distrust, and even the act of helping them to see this for themselves will forge trust in your leadership.

Your responsibility is to attune your senses to when *you yourself* experience systemic distrust.

By illuminating your own resistance points, you will naturally be able to see when this arises in the people that you lead.

Over time, you will develop an ability to help support your people past this covert resistance.

You will become a more trustworthy leader.

#2 – Distrust of Themselves

Most people are excellent at masking when they don't trust themselves. Let me give you an example.

I run a mastermind for high-caliber and high-character men called The Great Man Mastermind. For a period of 12 months, a select group of 20 men come together to identify their purpose and design a future they can't wait to live into.

Greg, a 43-year-old man I've known for over a decade, was a no brainer for this group. He's talented, loving, and brings positive energy everywhere he goes. He was also in a deep state of personal transition, feeling disconnected from purpose and isolated from deeper connections with other men.

Yet my repeated attempts to invite him into the group were met with lukewarm enthusiasm. Sometimes my texts would go unreturned.

I could have taken Greg's lack of responses as an affront to my leadership, but I knew on a deeper level that wasn't the case.

I can be very persistent, so I eventually got Greg on the phone and wouldn't let him disappear on me anymore.

He revealed to me that he was never ignoring me. He said this mastermind was exactly the thing he needed. But he feared signing up, failing to do the work, and subsequently disappointing himself, his wife, and me.

He didn't trust himself.

This was a pattern for him in all areas of his life that were of the utmost importance to him: his relationship with his wife and his kids, his work and his creative endeavors like writing and cooking.

I told him that the only way to break this pattern was to learn how to trust himself, and everything he's ever wanted was on the other side of that shift.

I asked Greg, "Can you trust yourself enough, in this moment, to identify that I'm a man you can trust to guide you through this shift?"

He did.

He joined The Great Man Mastermind and is fortifying his trust in himself every single day.

The people you lead will distrust themselves for the following two reasons:

1. ***Distrust in their ability to get the job done.***

   As was the case with Greg, this can carry a lot of shame. People will hide, make excuses, or disappear entirely to avoid the embarrassment they feel from having to admit they don't feel equipped to get the job done.

   Your job is to create safe environments where they can bring these feelings to you, without shame or embarrassment, and where you can assure them you will not let them fall.

2. ***Distrust in their ability to discern and believe in a leader who has their best interests at heart.***

   Chances are everyone you lead has been burned in the past by placing faith in a leader who took advantage of, disappointed, or even betrayed them.

   This causes them to doubt their own abilities to choose a trustworthy leader.

   The only way you overcome this distrust is by showing up, day in and day out, as an On Purpose Leader, to prove that they do in fact have the ability to discern and believe in a leader that has their best interests at heart.

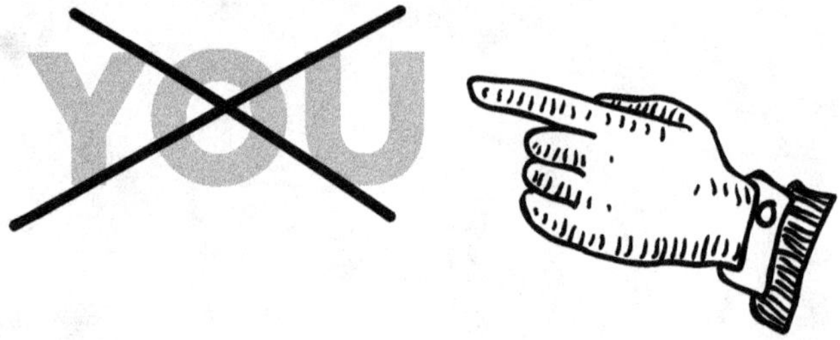

#3 – Distrust of You

The story at the start about Patrick getting passed over for the National Head of Sales job was a case study in "distrust of you."

As you can see from that story, it's often the little things that either erode or fortify trust in your leadership.

Drifting is what causes those "little things" to turn into tipping points of distrust over extended periods of time.

Drifting is a term borrowed from renowned author and teacher Napoleon Hill, used to describe a state of unconscious thinking, feeling, and behaving.

I wrote about this extensively in my first book, *Design Your*

Future: 3 Steps to Stop Drifting and Take Command of Your Life.

When you drift, you are Off Purpose.

You cannot drift and be On Purpose at the same time.

When you are drifting, you have relinquished intentionality and are operating on unconscious autopilot.

When you are drifting, you have strayed from one or more of the key tenets of the On Purpose Leader.

1. ***You're out of alignment with your Purpose.***
2. ***You've strayed from your Principles.***
3. ***You've broken from - or don't have - a Plan.***
4. ***You've stopped your Practices.***

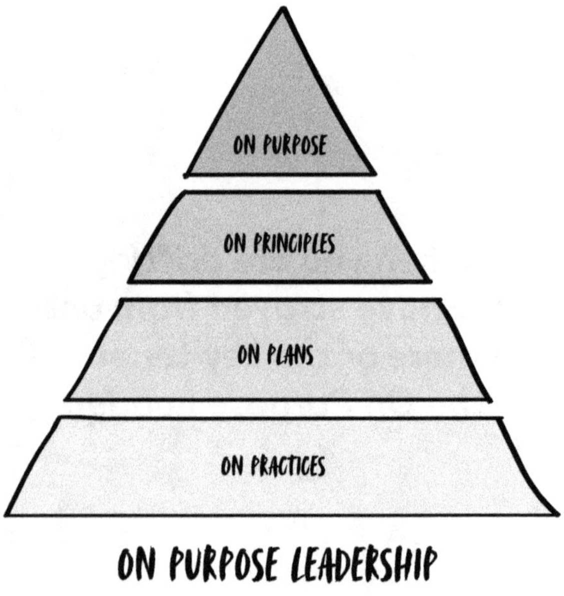

Any time you're feeling like you're operating below your standard – or experiencing resistance to your leadership – I want you to come back to these four tenets and see where you may be drifting.

Remember, you cannot be drifting and On Purpose at the same time.

You cannot be drifting and mastering the art of leading yourself at the same time.

You cannot be drifting and build trust in your leadership at the same time.

If you are drifting while leading yourself, it will eventually show up as erratic behavior or results on your team, a resistance to embracing change or an inability to execute.

Believe me, I've experienced all of these from my own failings in leadership.

You need to understand that drift is your number one enemy to mastering the art of leading yourself.

Drift is your number one enemy to becoming a more trustworthy leader.

The way to break free from drift is intentionality.

The dictionary definition of intentionality is "done on purpose."

Simple.

3

The Three Reasons Why People Will Distrust You

The people you lead will distrust you for the following three reasons:

1

Distrust in your ability to lead and achieve the desired results.

It's as simple as this:

Do the people you lead believe you can get the job done?

The answer to this will be on a spectrum. At one end you have Hell Yes. On the other end you have Hell No. And in the middle, you have Maybe.

As a leader, you are charged with the responsibility of taking people from where they are to where they want to go. Whether that's in business, in your family, in personal development...the buck stops with you when it comes to delivering results.

The effort you generate from the people you lead will be directly proportional to where you are on the spectrum.

The closer they feel to "hell yes" the more likely it is you can lead them to the desired results, the greater effort you will generate from the team.

2

Distrust in your ability to help them get what they want.

Many leadership situations involve a collective objective.

Underneath that collective objective, however, are a multitude of individual objectives.

For example, your business may have just posted record revenue. By that standard, the year is a success.

But each individual in the business has different dreams:

- » Upward career progression
- » Getting a fat bonus
- » Being recognized for extraordinary effort
- » Work-life balance
- » Investment in personal development

If you're hitting the collective goal at the expense or ignorance of their individual desires, your people will eventually come to distrust your ability to help them achieve what's most important to them.

Your followership will weaken, people will eventually stop going the extra mile for you, and discontent will spread like a cancer.

Here's a simple exercise to try.

Write down the name of every person you lead.

Next to their names, write down the answer to these questions:

» What is the number one most important driving force for this person?

» What are one to three things I can do to support this person in getting what they want?

Chances are you'll have a hard time truly knowing the first thing for every single person.

Even if you do feel confident that you do, be careful. If you haven't had explicit conversations about this precise thing with every person you lead, you may not be as accurate as you think.

I'd encourage you to establish a one-on-one meeting with each person to specifically focus on the number one most important thing they are working towards, even if it has nothing to do with the business at hand, and how you can help support them in their pursuit.

Then watch as the Trust in You meter goes on tilt.

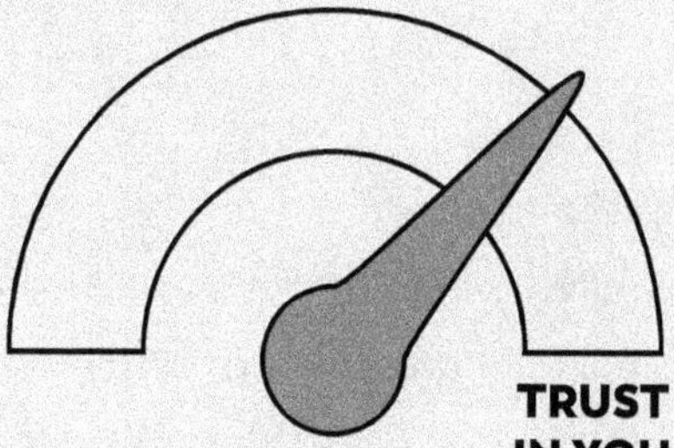

3

Distrust in whether you trust yourself

This is the big one.

We all transmit externally much or all of what we are feeling internally.

If there are seeds of doubt within you about your ability to lead, those around you will sense it and then come join your doubt party.

When you don't trust yourself:

- » You hesitate.
- » You second guess.
- » You fail to take bold, decisive action.
- » You fail to address subpar performance.
- » You fail to light a fire (because yours isn't burning).

On some level, we all struggle with this.

I know for me personally, in my younger years, this was my Achilles heel.

During high school sports and in my early 20s, I was afraid of the men I was in charge of leading.

When it came to "lead by example," I was the poster boy. But when I had to stand in front of a group of men and inspire them with my words, that was a whole new ballgame.

For example, my fraternity brothers in college thought enough of me to elect me their president, but I never commanded their full respect. There were other guys in the room who had bigger and more influential voices. I was intimidated by them, so I had trouble standing up to them because I feared confrontation with them. I didn't trust myself to go toe-to-toe with them. So every time I attempted to lead the meeting or the future of the fraternity in a direction that opposed the powerful brothers, I couldn't help but transmit my lack of trust in myself and would subsequently get steamrolled by those guys.

It was only when I learned to lead myself that I built inner fortitude. Now, the biggest compliment I receive from people I've just met is: "You carry yourself with this confidence that's both reassuring and disarming."

It's because I trust myself.

There's nothing more magnetic to other people than a leader who trusts him/herself.

On Purpose Leadership is the foundation on which you build Inner Trust in yourself.

IN SUMMARY

All resistance of your leadership is boiled down to one thing: distrust.

Distrust comes in three forms:

1. Distrust of *The System*
2. Distrust of *Themselves*
3. Distrust of *You*

While you are responsible for navigating all three of these, the one you have the most control over is #3: Distrust of You.

When you are drifting, you are Off Purpose. When you are Off Purpose, those you lead will doubt your ability to get the job done. They will wonder whether you have their best interests at heart. They will question whether you believe enough in yourself to succeed.

They will distrust you.

However, when you have the trust of those you lead, the sky is the limit when it comes to what you can accomplish.

The remainder of this book is designed to support you in mastering the art of leading yourself, which is the gateway to securing enduring trust from those you lead.

CHAPTER 2

ON PURPOSE

When you think about living "your purpose," what comes to mind?

When I ask my clients this question, the responses usually follow this thought pattern:

> *"It's the reason I'm here on this planet...but I don't know what it is."*
>
> *"I still need to find it."*
>
> *"Why can't I figure out my purpose?"*
>
> **Sigh of Despair**

When it comes to your purpose, you are likely making two key mistakes:

1. ***Believing purpose is some hidden thing that exists outside of yourself that you must venture far and wide to find.***

   We seem to have this prevailing belief that our purpose is locked away in some buried treasure chest that requires an Indiana Jones expedition to unlock.

   While that adventure might sound cool, purpose is actually much closer and far less dangerous to pursue.

2. ***Believing purpose must come in the form of a superhuman achievement that requires years, decades, or a lifetime to realize.***

   We've come to believe that purpose can only be acquired through the attainment of some distant, massive achievement like "impacting a billion lives" or "revolutionizing the financial services system" or "making sure a new Kardashian series never happens again."

While those are noble causes that the world certainly needs somebody to undertake, there's a little secret...

Feeling a regular sense of purpose is not about crushing massive goals or grinding away your life in the hopes of some far-off payoff.

Purpose only exists in the here and now, in the moment to moment of your existence.

In other words, living your purpose is not an achievement or an outcome; purpose is a feeling that's supported by aligned action.

This may be a bit esoteric for you right now, but we'll get much more specific in the next section on Your Greatest Energy.

For now, let's equip you with a clear definition of the two components of living On Purpose:

1. You are operating in your Greatest Energy.
2. You are surrounded by people who see your Highest Self.

When you are firing on both of these cylinders, you have mastered the art of leading yourself.

When you have mastered the art of leading yourself, leading others becomes so much easier.

So our first stop on this simple journey is my absolute favorite: finding what gives you your Greatest Energy.

YOUR GREATEST ENERGY

Brad Barrett is a humble guy who tends to avoid the spotlight. He still can't believe he's inspired a movement that's turned into a book, a documentary, a podcast with over 16 million downloads, and 300 community groups in nearly 300 cities around the world.

Brad's an old friend of mine – and straight-up good dude – from the University of Richmond.

After a 15-year hiatus, we reconnected in 2016 and established a monthly phone call ritual that we still maintain to this day. Brad also attended my very first Design Your Future men's retreat in March of 2017.

Back in 2013, Brad and his wife Laura, proudly frugal, were CPAs by day and had a particular passion for saving money.

As a family of four, they bought a home in Richmond, Virginia, and created a lifestyle where they managed their expenses down to an inconceivable $40,000 a year. Yes, you read that right: a home-owning family of four in a mid-sized American city for $40,000 a year.

Brad and Laura took pride in their meticulous saving and spending habits. While most Americans would find these perceived sacrifices as exhausting, Brad and Laura found this ***energizing***.

The Barrett's were living what's known as the Financial Independence (FI) lifestyle.

Its principles are straightforward:

1. Spend less.
2. Save more.
3. Invest the difference.
4. Work becomes an option, rather than a requirement.

Since Americans are crippled with debt and the FI movement was still pretty much underground at this time, Brad and Laura launched a side-hustle online business in the form of a blog called Richmond Savers.

It was simple: They taught people and families how to be smarter with their money.

For example, Brad and Laura were masters – Market Mavens, as Malcolm Gladwell might say – of the credit card points systems. They learned every in and out of how to leverage those "get 50,000 points to sign up by signing up for the Capitol One Venture One" deals. So they created a business model around educating consumers on how to squeeze the most value out of their miles.

Richmond Savers would regularly feature a credit card on the website that Brad and Laura had vetted and approved. Each time a user would sign up through Richmond Savers, Brad and Laura would earn an affiliate fee.

It was a modest, albeit solid and growing, income stream that showed promise.

Then, Brad took it a step further and was inspired to write an article entitled "Take Your Family to Disney World For Free: Step-by-Step Instructions."

It went viral.

In early 2014, his article was featured in the *New York Times*, on NBC and CBS, and his website traffic blew up.

Brad knew he was onto something. He was inspired to share more, so he followed that energy and kept going.

In February of 2015, Brad launched "Travel Miles 101," a free online course that teaches you how to maximize your card points for travel. Over 50,000 people have been through this course since inception.

Brad still felt like he had yet more to share, so in late 2016, he did that "follow the energy" thing again.

He started a podcast with a local buddy of his, Jonathan Mendonsa, who had paid off over $168,000 in student loan debt and had a similar passion for the financial independence lifestyle. Together, they began to spread the word to everyday Americans about how they could take back control of their financial lives.

On December 18th, 2016, the *ChooseFI* (Choose Financial Independence) podcast launched with its first episode: "A Finance Podcast for the Middle Class."

The show immediately caught fire.

Three years later, the *ChooseFI* podcast has over 16 million downloads.[2] It also has a vibrantly active Facebook group of over 60,000 members, 300 community and cohort groups in nearly 300 cities all over the world, a book with its name, and a feature in the financial independence documentary *Playing With FIRE.*

Most importantly, the spotlight they've shined on the principles of FI is changing people's lives.

I've been honored to be a two-time guest on the ChooseFI podcast and had a chance to meet some of their community members at the *Playing With FIRE* documentary screening in Times Square.

Their community is *rabid*, and I mean that in the best of ways. These people are passionate, educated, and virtually drift-free when it comes to how intentionally they're building their financial futures.

---

2 As of January 2020.

Brad and Jonathan are revolutionary people who are turning the tides of financial wellbeing in this country, and the world.

Way back in 2013 when Brad first started, he had no master plan. He didn't declare "sharing financial independence is my life's purpose"; he simply followed what gave him his Greatest Energy.

Your Greatest Energy is your portal to living On Purpose.

Finding Your Greatest Energy

As *Rich Dad, Poor Dad* author Robert Kiyosaki says, "You have something special inside of you."

The evidence of this is when you are in your Greatest Energy.

It's that sensation of being fully online, inspired, and determined.

Your Greatest Energy is never in the future; it's only available in the here and now.

For example, Brad's meteoric rise from humble middle-class American to global impact did not come because of some master plan or expedition to find the elusive "purpose."

He followed what gave him his energy.

» He loved saving his money and watching his bank account grow.

» He loved being a contrarian to the typical American spending and savings habits.

» He loved uncovering hidden travel deals.

» He loved the idea of achieving financial independence decades before normal retirement age.

» He loved sharing what he was learning with others.

When you're doing what gives you your Greatest Energy:

1. You feel a sense of selflessness, timelessness, and effortlessness.
2. You feel connected to something bigger than yourself.
3. You come home energized, not exhausted, from doing whatever it is, all day long.

Sometimes these things have *seemingly* nothing to do with the job that you get paid for.

I would argue that it has *everything* to do with what you get paid for; you simply haven't connected the dots yet.

The funny thing about your Greatest Energy is it refuses to remain compartmentalized, meaning if you experience your Greatest Energy in one context of your life, it will eventually demand to get bigger and grow into other contexts.

A simple example from my life was when I rekindled my long-lost love affair with reading books.

Back in 2009, after a 20-year hiatus, I started reading again.

I dove headfirst into personal development, mindfulness,

and spiritual texts. I'd get lost in these adventures to unfamiliar worlds. Time would slip away, and it was like I'd been transported to another dimension of high-octane learning. At times, it felt like infinite wisdom was being downloaded into my inner operating system like Neo in *The Matrix*.

On the surface, the books I was reading didn't seem to be entirely relevant to the financial services industry. This was something I did on my own time, so I viewed it in the compartment of "personal."

But eventually something was sparked inside of me to start sharing the key lessons I'd learned from these books in the workplace.

As is the case in most industries, very few people tend to seek information outside the pale of their business niche, so what I was sharing was novel, intriguing, and valuable.

Over time, I became a trusted resource known as the go-to guy for book recommendations.

My personal brand evolved into someone who was a "big-picture thinker" and regularly found myself tapped for exciting strategic discussions and innovation exercises that gave me exposure to Prudential Retirement's top brass.

What started as following my Greatest Energy – developing myself through reading books – turned into an accelerator for my professional career.

At age 30, I was promoted from my individual contributor sales role into a prestigious leadership position – running the East Coast sales team with a $1.4 billion sales goal.

I attribute that quick ascension in great part to following my Greatest Energy.

Here's the important thing to understand: *You do not need to know the endgame of following your Greatest Energy.*

Think of it like reading a book. If the story is captivating, you'll keep reading even if you don't know how it ends, right?

That's the same thing with your Greatest Energy.

The more time you spend operating from that space, the more alive and vibrant you will feel, and that will amplify the impact you have in all areas of your life.

Follow your Spark

But what if you don't know what gives you your Greatest Energy?

Well, first, you need to follow your spark.

Just like Sam did.

Sam is a client of mine. He is 50 years old, married with three kids, and runs a $1-billion-in-annual-revenue division for a Fortune 250 company.

He's universally respected and sits atop all of the organization charts, including the big one: president.

In a rare moment of candor, he expressed a phenomenon that many men experience: *Disconnection from and not knowing what brings you energy.*

I asked him, "What have you been dreaming about doing that you've yet to try?"

After a few beats, he said, "I've always been curious about yoga."

Within the next two weeks, he'd hired a personal yoga instructor who guided him through private virtual classes in his home over the computer.

According to the yoga teacher, who's a friend of mine, he's an exceptionally gifted student.

Sam is unlikely to become a yoga teacher in this lifetime, but the benefits are undeniable:

- He feels a new sense of growth and aliveness in his life.
- His curiosity to learn more has been sparked in other areas.

He feels a deeper sense of peace and joy in his daily living.

All of these benefits contribute to his showing up as a better leader.

It's that easy to kickstart new ideas to find your spark.

If you find yourself in the same place as where Sam started, here's your protocol for that:

1. **Generate Ideas Like a Think Tank**
   Pretend you're an innovation think tank (for yourself) and generate as many ideas as you can. You're going for quantity over quality at first. If you're not coming up with any hair-brained ideas, you're being too boring. Test ideas in your mind (take improv, commit to Toastmasters, take a six-week online personal finance course) until something lands to you as a "now that sounds cool."

2. **Stop Thinking and Just Do It**
   The trap we fall into is overthinking and overanalyzing. Stop staring at the pool; jump in the water and give it a swim. Tom Bilyeu, founder of Quest, the $1 billon protein bar company said it best: "I'd rather run 200 miles an hour in the wrong direction than stand still,

because being in motion gives me valuable feedback on where the right next direction is."

3. **Refine and Do It Again**
   If you try something and it doesn't spark, great, you've just collected invaluable data on what doesn't work. Channel your inner Thomas Edison and go back and test another approach. If you caught a spark, what did you learn about yourself about why that particular thing gave you energy? Take that insight and either double down on what you're already doing or use it to seek the next spark.

And if you still need a kick-start, try the next simple exercise to get you going.

FIND YOUR SPARK

1. What do you find yourself daydreaming about doing that you haven't tried yet or have been postponing?
2. What's a meaningful part of you that you haven't been sharing with the world?
3. What's a new practice you can implement every day that'll take you under 10 minutes of time?
4. How can you make your next trip more of an adventure (unpredictable, novel, high possibility for growth) vs. a vacation (predictable, relaxing, but potentially more of the same)?
5. What are the physical and emotional sensations you experience when you feel a spark? Where in your body do you feel them?

Aligning Your Life

What would it feel like if you aligned your entire life around living in your Greatest Energy?

This doesn't mean throwing away the career you've spent a lifetime building.

It means finding your Greatest Energy where you are and relentlessly seeking to increase the amount of time you spend in your Greatest Energy. Play the long game.

One of my clients, Steve Wilt, is one of the nation's most prolific and well-respected financial advisors in the retirement services space. He loves helping companies build retirement plans that allow Americans to retire safely and securely.

After three decades at the top of his field, Steve was seeking a new challenge, an injection of new purpose-driven energy. So he decided to come to one of my men's retreats.

I soon learned Steve is an elite public speaker who derives tremendous joy from being on stage. In fact, he cited a 10-minute keynote speech that he gave at the closing of his firm's national sales conference as one of his "peak professional moments," which is code for Greatest Energy.

So I pushed him to find his way onto more stages. He quickly found his way onto the stage of the industry's largest annual conference, with over 2,000 people in the audience.

I was there.

He crushed it.

Steve is a man on fire.

By organizing more of his life around what gives him his energy; his business has elevated along with him.

I actually want you to put the book down for 60 seconds and contemplate living a life where you've organized 100 percent of your life around doing the things that give you your Greatest Energy.

Don't limit yourself with practicality or present-day constraints.

Just dream for 60 seconds.

Now I want you to ask yourself the following three questions:

1. On a scale of 0% to 100%, how much of your present life is aligned around living in your Greatest Energy?
2. If you were to upgrade by 10%, what benefits would you expect to experience in your life?
3. What changes do you need to make, right now, that can help you upgrade by 10%?

There are plenty of things that you're doing right now that are clogging the pipes through which your Greatest Energy wants to flow.

To explain what I mean, one of my friends and mentors, the digital marketing genius George Bryant, has a simple and useful exercise.

What are the three things you hate doing, but you always end up doing them?

1. ____________

2. ____________

3. ____________

Any time you spend doing these three things you hate is time spent stealing from your Greatest Energy.

Once you've come up with your list, you have three choices:

1. Keep doing them

2. Delete them

3. Delegate them

For example, one of my clients hates cleaning her house and doing the laundry after a 60-hour workweek, but the tasks always seemed to fall to her.

I pushed her to hire a housekeeper. She grew up in a humble household where there wasn't a lot of money, so hiring a housekeeper felt extravagant and self-indulgent.

But when we reframed the issue as an "every moment you spend washing underwear is a moment you are robbing yourself from your Greatest Energy," she had an awakening.

Hiring a housekeeper became one of the best decisions of her life.

When you align 100 percent of your life around your Greatest Energy, you show up in the world energized, alive, and sharing your greatest gifts with everyone around you.

Who wouldn't want to follow a leader like that?

Those Who See Your Highest Self

Now that you have thought about what gives you energy, you need to think about who gives you energy.

There are three types of people in your life, but only one of them calls you forward to living your highest self.

This special type of person can be the difference between you settling for mediocrity or living a life people will be talking about long after you're gone.

To best illustrate the three types of people in your life – and the criticality of having the special one – I'd like to tell you a story about one of the most important people in my life, my sister Mary.

Mary loves smiling, bowling, and is generally unbeatable at Yahtzee. She calls me Domino, a nickname she finds still finds hilarious, even after 41 years.

Undisputedly, she gives the world's warmest hugs. Her favorite color is pink, as evidenced by her bedroom where it looks like a case of Pepto Bismol has exploded.

More than anything in this world, she loves babies.

In family circles, she's known as the "Baby Whisperer," as no crying baby has ever outlasted my sister's patience or calming embrace.

Although she has never been diagnosed with a learning difficulty like autism or Down Syndrome, Mary is different; you'd say, "special needs."

From an early age, medical professionals and special needs experts started bracing my parents for the reality that Mary would always require a lifetime of extra care.

She would never be able to live on her own, hold a regular job, or be fully independent.

Growing up, I witnessed how hard Mary's differences were on her.

Mary was a grade above me. From Kindergarten to sixth grade, we went to different schools. She went to Smith (public) while I went to St. Paul's (Catholic), so I didn't witness her hardships firsthand. Instead, I'd see her when she came home.

Kids can be tough. More than a few times, Mary would come home despondent. Sometimes in tears. She'd be teased for talking to herself in the hallways, looking disheveled, or eating alone.

Teachers could be tough too. Mary split her time between mainstream and special education classes. During parent-teacher conferences, mainstream teachers were quick to point Mary's limitations and low-future ceilings, although they were probably just trying to be realistic.

That was until she got a new eight-grade teacher, Mrs. Unrath.

Mrs. Unrath's reputation preceded her. She was notoriously the hardest-assed, most unforgiving teacher in Smith School. She was legendary for pop quizzes, chewing out students who didn't come prepared and... worst of all...calling on you spontaneously in class.

This worried my mother. Mary had never thrived when put on the spot, and my mother forecasted a long year of torment for my sister.

So my mother reached out to Mrs. Unrath shortly before the school year began and explained Mary's situation.

"Give me a week with your daughter in class," Mrs. Unrath said. "And I'll be back in touch."

The following week, my mother's phone rang.

"Your daughter has a processing delay," Mrs. Unrath said.

That's strange, my mother thought. After years of having Mary tested by medical professionals, no one had ever suggested "processing delay" with her learning challenges.

Mrs. Unrath explained:

> With a few adjustments, I believe Mary can function at a high level in this classroom. Mary shows solid comprehension on the work that's in front of her. It just takes her longer to complete.
>
> She needs time to process information. So instead of putting her on the spot in class, I've coordinated a signal with Mary to let her know a question is coming her way. When I put my hand on her desk, she knows that the next question is for her. And I will give her extra time before calling on her for the answer.
>
> I also tutor four nights a week. If you make sure Mary is here for two of those nights, I guarantee she will be mainstream math come high school.

My mother was flooded with emotions, including both excitement and fear...but above all, hope.

No teacher had ever believed in Mary like this before. Especially not after one week. Especially not the hardest-assed, most unforgiving teacher in the school.

So, with trepidation, my mother agreed to Mrs. Unrath's plan, and she sent Mary off to a year in her classroom.

At the end of the final semester, *Mary finished the year with a B average.*

She was mainstreamed for high school math.

Just like Mrs. Unrath guaranteed.

Today, 28 years after Mrs. Unrath came into our lives, Mary is 42 years old, living on her own, and has held a steady job for nearly two decades.

Being mainstreamed in her high school education meant Mary could graduate and enroll in a community college where she studied early childhood development.

Her college degree enabled her to land a job at a day care center, secure a steady paycheck, and eventually, her own apartment.

Over a decade ago, Mary took up residence at The Woodlands, a senior citizen's home in the town where my family still lives. Ten percent of the subsidized units are available for non-senior citizens who are classified with "disabilities."

It seemed like an odd pairing at first, but Mary couldn't have landed in a better place.

She has finally found a community of people who embrace her.

Because as it turns out, Mary's natural born skills as a (very) patient listener are valuable currency in a place where people have no shortage of stories or time.

She's a regular at the card-game tables, more than holding her own at old-school games like Pokeno and Canasta.

She's even turned into the resident technology whiz. Need to set up an Amazon Alexa or FaceTime your grandson? Mary's your woman.

Mary is now the longest tenured employee – 18 years on the job – at The Goddard School, a daycare center where she cares for infants six weeks to 12 months of age.

Her gentle, loving touch has nurtured hundreds of babies – and reassured nearly twice as many parents – during the most fragile moments of the newborns' lives.

Her skills as The Baby Whisperer found a perfect home.

She lives every day, On Purpose.

I once asked Mary how many diapers she changes per day.

Conservatively, at least 10, she estimates.

After 18 years on the job, that equates to roughly 32,400 diaper changes, according to my math.

When I tell her this, her eyes light up, and she laughs...as she often does.

There was a time when Mary was underestimated by nearly everyone...doctors, experts, even her family.

It took the intervention of one special educator – Mrs. Dorothy Unrath – to step in and see the potential in Mary that everyone overlooked.

Succeeding in Mrs. Unrath's class seemed like a small, albeit significant, win at the time...

But what it really represented was a new, upward-pointing trajectory for Mary's life *that changed everything.*

Do you have a Mrs. Unrath in your life?

THE THREE TYPES OF PEOPLE IN YOUR LIFE

There are three types of people in your life, but only one of them calls you forward to living the greatest version of yourself, like Mrs. Unrath was for my sister Mary.

People see you in one of three ways:

1. **The "Then" Version of You:** These are the people who cling to an antiquated version of you. They themselves are likely stuck in the past and don't want to acknowledge who you've become. Your progress is threatening to them because they fear you leaving them behind.

2. **The "Now" Version of You:** These are the people who see you as you are today – your current job, skill sets, marital status, financial status, physical appearance, etc. They are supportive of this version of you. They may even encourage your progress, as long as it's not too big, bold, or dramatic. Too much change too quickly scares them, for fear of losing the version of you they wish to cling to.

3. **The "Highest" Version of You:** That rare breed of person who sees past your present-day greatness and limitations and only speaks to the most elevated version of who you are, and who you can become. Like Mrs. Unrath.

In my experience, *up to 95 percent of the people in your life fall into the second category.*

Here are the problems with that.

These people often can't or won't call you forward into what gives you your Greatest Energy. They value stability and homeostasis over growth.

As you play the game of aligning 100 percent of your life around your Greatest Energy, you will start to elevate. Fast. You will change. Your life will change.

This will be destabilizing for some of the people in your life, and they may resist your growth.

This is where the third category of people are essential – the people who see and encourage the highest version of you.

Here's what they do best:

» They see past the "now" version of you and can speak directly to your best self.

» They hold you to the standard of the highest version of you and won't allow you to shrink.

» They will call you on your bullshit excuses and see right through you when you try to package up a B+ and pass it off like an A.

» They can often see a higher version of you than you can see for yourself.

» They catch you when you're Off Purpose and guide you back On Purpose.

You need people in your life who will be the catalysts for some of your deepest, fastest, and most profound growth, ever.

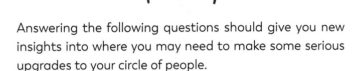

Answering the following questions should give you new insights into where you may need to make some serious upgrades to your circle of people.

CHOOSE THE PEOPLE IN YOUR LIFE

1. Using the "Three Types of People in Your Life," categorize the five to ten people you spend the most time with.
2. Is there one person in your life who is holding you back and you need to cut ties with?
3. Who are the people giving you your Greatest Energy (beyond your partner/spouse)?
4. When was the last time you intentionally sought out a great relationship in your life, versus waiting for it to come to you?
5. Who are three to five people in your life that you can deepen or forge new relationships with?

You cannot leave finding people who give you your Greatest Energy to chance.

My sister Mary got lucky with Mrs. Unrath. But luck is not strategy.

If you want to increase the percentage and impact of great people in your life, you need to make an intentional decision to seek out and cultivate these relationships.

Need ideas to do that?

1. **Ask someone to be your mentor**

   When you do, tell them why you've chosen them and recognize them for the important role they play in your life.

   Tell them how you plan to be an exceptional mentee and ask them what they would need to feel energized about the relationship.

2. **Pay a coach**

   If you've never had a coach before, you have no idea how powerful it is to have someone exclusively dedicated to focusing on you and you only during your time together.

A good coach only sees the highest version of you and literally gets paid to hold you to that standard.

Over the last decade I've rarely gone longer than a few months without a paid coach. It's really hard to drift Off Purpose and shrink from the highest version of myself when I have someone regularly on my ass.

3. Ask someone to start a mastermind with you

Here's one way to invite in someone great into your life: Ask them. Directly.

A mastermind is a group that comes together for a common definite purpose. For example:

» Becoming better fathers

» Achieving financial independence

» Mastering public speaking

There's tremendous flexibility in the frequency in the design of a mastermind, including the frequency with which you meet. Some masterminds meet weekly, others meet quarterly or even annually.

The important point is to invite people who speak to the Highest You and design the mastermind around it.

When you make the invitation, use words to this effect:

You're someone who calls me forward to a higher standard and inspires me to live the greatest version of myself. Thank you for being such an important part of my life.

I'd love to continue to call each other forward in work and in life. I'd like to invite you to join me in creating a mastermind with the intention of living the best version of ourselves. Are you in?

As you cultivate better relationships in your life, you will also become a better person for more of the people in your life, including those you lead.

Isn't that what we all want?

IN SUMMARY

The two components of living On Purpose:

1. You are operating in your Greatest Energy.
2. You are surrounded by people who see your Highest Self.

When you've mastered the art of leading yourself On Purpose, you will naturally become a more trustworthy leader that others will be inspired to follow.

But as we know, drift is a powerful force that inevitably seduces us off track.

We must fortify our strength against such a diversion.

An essential tenet in doing so is designing the Principles that guide your life and leadership, which we will explore next.

CHAPTER 3

ON PRINCIPLES

Tony Hayward was the hair-brained CEO of BP during the catastrophic oil spill of 2010.

After a tragic and fatal explosion on the Deepwater Horizon, 210 million gallons of crude oil was pumped into the Gulf of Mexico over an 87-day period, making it the largest marine oil spill in the history of the petroleum industry.

For some reason, Hayward didn't find this to be a big deal. He publicly stated:

> The Gulf of Mexico is a very big ocean. The amount of volume of oil and dispersant we are putting into it is tiny in relation to the total water volume.

> I think the environmental impact of this disaster is likely to be very, very modest.

If you want a textbook example of what the abdication of leadership looks like, there it is.

He had quite a few public relations doozies like this.

His most infamous one was when he turned his company's inability to stem the environmental disaster into a "woe is me" moment: *"There's no one who wants this over more than I do.* ***I'd like my life back."***

Calling Hayward's petulant response "tone deaf" would be an understatement, considering 11 BP employees literally lost their lives in the oil rig explosion, and he was complaining about the inconvenience of having to clean up his own mess.

Hayward was eviscerated by the media, and customers refused to patronize BP's gas stations (I was one of them).

By October 1, 2010, Tony Hayward was no longer CEO of BP.

Clearly, Tony Hayward did not rely upon any guiding principles during this "war time" disaster scenario.

Let's juxtapose the BP oil spill fiasco with what can happen when leaders rely upon intentionally designed **principles** to guide their behaviors in the most chaotic of situations.

In 1982, Tylenol was the sacred cow of Johnson & Johnson's product portfolio.

At the time, Tylenol accounted for 19% of J&J's corporate profits, and it outsold it's top four competitors – Anacin, Bayer, Buffer and Excedrin – *combined.*

If Tylenol were a standalone business, it's profits would have placed it in the Fortune 250.

And then, in 1982, a disturbed individual decided to start slipping cyanide-laced capsules into the Tylenol Extra Strength containers.[3]

Seven unsuspecting consumers were tragically killed.

Suddenly, Tylenol found itself sucker punched and reeling on its heels from a massive public relations nightmare, having to respond to and defend why its trusted product was now killing innocent civilians.

---

3 - Or group of individuals, as the perpetrator was never caught.

Throughout the crisis, over 100,000 separate news stories ran in US newspapers, making it the widest-covered US news story since the assassination of President John F. Kennedy.[4]

Johnson & Johnson chairman, James Burke, immediately formed a seven-member strategy team with two questions that served as guiding principles for disaster protocol:

1. "How do we protect the people?"

2. "How do we save this product?"

Notice which of those guiding principles came first, and which came second.

This distinction of priority is ultimately what most experts attribute J&J's ability to not only save its number one brand but also come out the other side thriving.

Johnson & Johnson made the tough decision to direct the public to immediately cease all consumption and purchase of Tylenol products until the extent of the contamination could be determined.

---

4 - Kaplin, 1998.

According to the *New York Times*, this decision cost the company $100 million.[5]

But J&J stood firm in their commitment to protecting the people (principle #1), which they also knew would ultimately protect the product (principle #2).

They also established a 1-800 hotline to support customer concerns and field questions.

Six months later, Tylenol became the first company ever to produce tamper-resistant packaging to the market.

According to the Department of Defense case study on crisis management:

> Scholars have come to recognize Johnson & Johnson's handling of the Tylenol crisis as the example for success when confronted with a threat to an organization's existence.
>
> Berge lauds the case in the following manner: "The Tylenol crisis is without a doubt the most exemplary case ever known in the history of crisis communications.

---

5 - That's over a quarter of a billion dollars in today's economy.

> "Any business executive, who has ever stumbled into a public relations ambush, ought to appreciate the way Johnson & Johnson responded to the Tylenol poisonings. They have effectively demonstrated how major business has to handle a disaster."

This very well could have been a death knell for Tylenol.

And yet, because of Johnson & Johnson's leadership's handling of the crisis, following its own guiding principles, Tylenol was able to restore faith with the public and full recover its market share.

Your life and your leadership will be tested in the most unpredictable and stressful ways.

When push comes to shove, what foundation will you stand upon to keep you On Purpose?

Will you be swept away into abdicating your leadership responsibilities like Tony Hayward of BP?

Or will you remain firmly rooted in your guiding principles like the executive leadership team at Tylenol?

The principles of an On Purpose Leader serve as your foundation and roots – your anti-drift devices – to weather any storm and lead with integrity.

The definition of a principle is: *"A fundamental truth or proposition that serves as the foundation for a system of belief or behavior or for a chain of reasoning."*

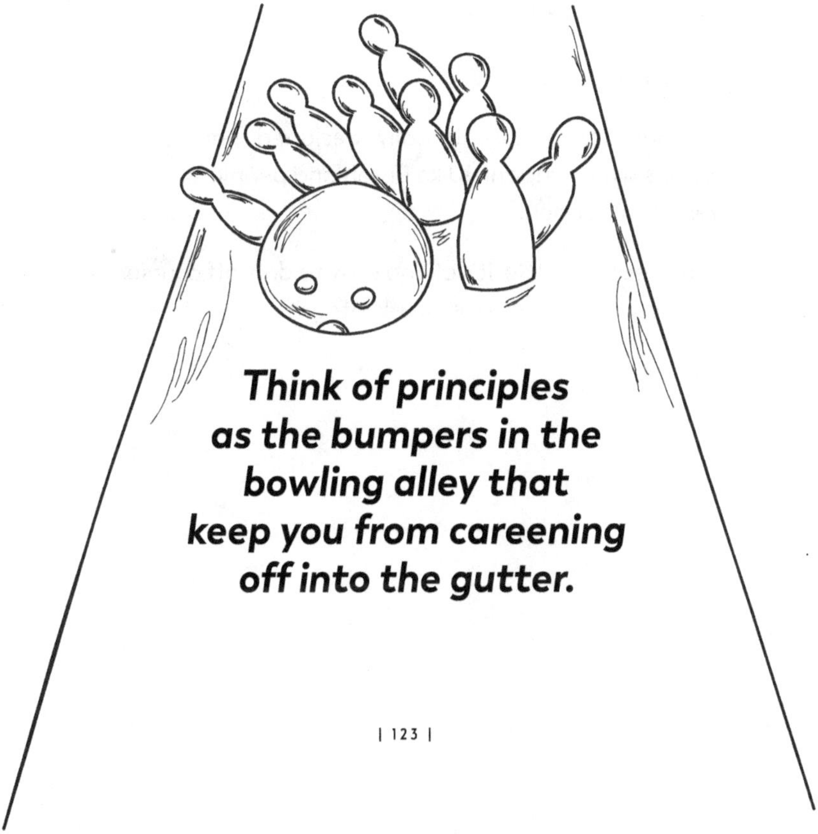

Think of principles as the bumpers in the bowling alley that keep you from careening off into the gutter.

The entire philosophy in Jocko Willink and Leif Babson's New York Times bestselling leadership book *Extreme Ownership* hinges on principles developed by the NAVY Seals. Here are some examples:

» *Extreme Ownership: The leader must own everything in his or her world.*

» *There are no bad teams, only bad leaders.*

» *Check the ego.*

The absence of intentionally designed principles are reasons why companies like Enron and people like Harvey Weinstein happen.

In the heat of battle, it's all too easy to drift off course, cut corners, pass blame, and break integrity.

On Purpose Leaders, however, subscribe to a defined set of principles where intentionality and integrity guide every behavior.

THE THREE PRINCIPLES OF ON PURPOSE LEADERSHIP

As you can see, the concept of principles can be leveraged to guide and govern your entire life, if you so choose.

For our purposes, we're going to simplify the universe of potential principles to just three.

Principle #1: Master the Art of Leading Yourself Before Leading Others

Let me explain this one with a *Harvard Business Review* case study.

International Power's seven-person senior management team finally decided to get serious about the thing every business complains about but rarely ever takes serious measures to change:

Email.

Email is the bane of nearly every modern professional's

existence, and International Power saw it as a threat to their efficiency as a business.

The leadership team viewed email like a manufacturing process, and there are two threats to manufacturing:

1. **Overproduction:** Is there anything more overproduced than email?

2. **Defects:** Unclear emails, emails that should have been phone calls, emails sent to people who didn't need to receive them, etc.

They knew they needed to clean up their mess.

Most leadership teams would likely look to their employee population's email habits and devise a company-wide campaign to transform their behavior. Instead, the executive team decided to lead themselves through behavior change before asking anything different of their employees.

International Power's leadership team underwent a training process where they learned to send fewer and better emails.

Within three months, the seven-person leadership team was sending 54% fewer emails.

That was a big win, but where it gets really interesting is the impact this behavior change created at the levels below them.

The 73 employees at the levels below the leadership team – who received zero training – started sending 64% fewer emails.

According to *Harvard Business Review*, this resulted in an annual gain of 10,400 staff-hours and a 7% increase in productivity, which were both sustained in the two years of follow-up after the case study was released.

All because the leaders looked at themselves first and asked, "How can we lead ourselves to mastery before we ask our people to do so?"

I love this case study from International Power because of its powerful implications.

» **Your behavior as a leader is amplified at the levels below you.**

In the case of International Power, one email an executive sent turned into hundreds of emails at the levels below. As soon as the leader changed their behavior, that behavior changed without any formal training or cumbersome new policy that would be nearly impossible to enforce.

The same holds true for other behaviors at the leadership level. If a leader transmits lack of clarity in his/her vision, lack of follow through on commitments or lack of integrity, you better believe these behaviors will be amplified at the layers below.

Conversely, a leader who communicates clear vision, delivers with meticulous execution and embodies integrity will infuse these behaviors into the people he or she leads.

» **You are either coaching it or allowing it to happen.**

In 2014, the Miami Dolphins NFL football team was embroiled in a bullying scandal that happened between teammates in the locker room. When Herm Edwards, a head football coach and ESPN analyst at the time was asked who was ultimately accountable for the scandal, he pointed at the head coach: *"Either you're coaching the behavior, or you're allowing it happen."*

I love this.

When the people you lead aren't executing, it's either because you yourself aren't executing (coaching it), or you're not putting the proper accountability protocols in place (allowing it to happen).

This aligns with the principle of Extreme Ownership: "The leader must own everything in his or her world."

» **In the end, you only have total control over changing your own behavior.**

As a leader, you have an ability to influence another person's behavior, but you only ever have total control over your own.

Therefore, your fastest, most reliable, and most impactful way to lead others to the behavior you expect of them is to lead yourself into embodying that behavior first.

Instead of asking: "How can I get others to change?"

Ask: "How can I change?"

Principle #2: Everyone Wants to Be Led

When Sallie Krawcheck was in her thirties, she was brought in to turn around Smith Barney, which was reeling from the equity research scandals and Nasdaq market meltdown.

When she was in her forties, she was brought in to turn around Merrill Lynch after the sub-prime mortgage disaster.

In both instances, the financial advisors at those

businesses were mostly male (around 85 percent) and in their late fifties to early sixties on average.

In other words, she didn't look anything like them or the leaders they were used to having.

Skepticism of her and her ability to lead ran rampant among the ranks.

Remember, distrust is the number one reason why people resist leadership, and these advisors did not trust Sallie.

In her article, "What I Learned About Leadership from the Skeptics," Sallie details her process of earning the trust of these advisors through communication, care, and being damn good at understanding the business. She says:

> I remember going to one of my first meetings, in which they all sat well back in their chairs, arms crossed. No smiles.
>
> What was immediately apparent: No matter what I did, I wasn't going to "be like them."
>
> Instead of acting like them, I set out from the very beginning to listen to them — a lot. It was to make sure they "felt heard."

As much as they'd never want to admit it, the resistors wanted to be led. But they needed to know not only that Sallie had the business chops but also that she cared.

Over time, she won over the skeptics and engineered remarkable turnarounds for Smith Barney and Merrill Lynch.

Krawcheck is now the CEO and co-founder of Ellevest, a digital financial advisor for women, and she's been recognized by Forbes as number seven on The World's 100 Most Powerful Women.

I remember something similar happening at Prudential Retirement, when our charismatic male leader left for a competitor and Christine Marcks became the first woman president of our business.

She was soft spoken, introverted, and bookish. There were rumors that her predominantly male type-A executive team grumbled about their doubts that she could effectively lead our business.

Her approach was to find new markets that none of our competitors had the foresight or acumen to play in. She made bold bets and saw them through.

While the rest of the industry was fighting off shrinking margins over a ten-year period of contraction, our business grew.

What Christine did over the decade of her tenure was lead Prudential – and her resistors – to become one of the most profitable and respected providers in the retirement services industry.

Leading is hard work.

Despite all of that, the reality is this:

***Everyone does,
in fact,
want to be led.***

I mean, ask yourself, if this book can help elevate your own leadership style, would you not gladly follow its guidance? (Of course; that's why you're here.)

People want to be led for these three reasons:

1. **Better With You:** They believe you can lead them to something better than they could get on their own.
2. **Faster With You:** They believe you can help them get it faster.
3. **Impossible Without You:** They believe they can't get it without you.

Of course, there's a premium on the last point, but there always has been and always will be a market for leadership that can deliver on any of those three reasons.

Think of the best leaders you ever had:

» What did they help teach you about yourself that you couldn't have learned on your own?

» What did they help you achieve that you couldn't have on your own (or at least helped you achieve much quicker)?

» What did you previously believe to be impossible that their leadership helped make possible for you?

Looking back, wasn't it a privilege to be led by the person(s) who led you to this higher ground?

Therefore, your responsibility as a leader is to know "the why" of each person you lead.

When you know their "why," and they trust in your ability to help lead them there, they will follow you.

Principle #3: Create Environments Where You and Those You Lead Can Thrive

One of the top 10 books of my life is *King, Warrior, Magician,* Lover by Robert Moore.

In the book, he describes the "king archetype" and the three duties of a king:

1. **Ordering:** Creating the vision for your kingdom, establishing and enforcing the rules and values, and organizing the assets of your kingdom in a way that puts everyone in position to thrive.
2. **Fertility:** Creating an ecosystem of generativity and prosperity where love, wealth, and opportunity flourish.
3. **Blessings:** Recognizing, acknowledging, and developing the people, their special gifts, and their valuable actions of those in your kingdom.

To make these practical to the world of business, these three duties of a leader can be renamed:

1. ***Vision and Culture***
2. ***Growth***
3. ***Talent Development***

The first part of this principle – *create an environment where you can thrive* – urges you to start with you first. It's the same thing as the overused analogy of putting on your own oxygen mask first.

The second part of this principle – *where those you lead can thrive* – is a charge for you to build an ecosystem where everyone flourishes.[6]

Your role as an On Purpose Leader carrying out this principle ensures:

---

6 - Think of this as the opposite of how the Lannisters in Game of Thrones ruled the Westerlands.

- Everyone, including you, thrives.
- No free rides for anyone on the backs of others.
- You actively seek out inequities and look to make them right.
- You ensure non-dominant groups thrive.
- Your kingdom is strong, secure, and flourishing.

For example, many male-dominated businesses – like financial services, law and technology – have created longstanding environments where women and people of color have not thrived.

Having spent 15 years in financial services myself, I was blind to the many privileges I received as a white man in a business where 70 percent of the leadership positions were held by people who looked like me.[7]

Would I have advanced as quickly or gotten the same opportunities to bond with leaders if 70 percent had been women?

Would Christine Marcks or Sallie Krawcheck have faced the same scrutiny if they were named Rick?[8]

---

7 - At least 70 percent!

---

8 - That's an inside joke for my *Great Man Within podcast listeners.*

The unfortunate truth is that when most majority groups have the numbers, the power, and the unfair share of benefits, there's usually very little interest in exploring the inequities that non-majority groups are experiencing.

Three years ago, I made a conscious decision to expand my perspective and seek guidance from groups of people who didn't look like me.

For example, I've gotten involved with a number of women's advocacy groups, like Women in Pension Network, One More Woman, and the Global League of Women.

By asking questions and listening intently, I've learned that very few men have made an adequate effort to educate themselves on how we can become better advocates of women in the workplace.

As I listened and learned, women felt heard. They showed me what I needed to do to be a better advocate and how to confront inequities and balance the playing field.

I gained trust with women's groups, eventually being asked to speak and facilitate workshops at women-only events.

In late 2019, I ended up running my own three-day women's retreat for seven vice president and senior vice president women in New York City. That led to a series of subsequent retreats and speaking engagements across the country in 2020.

So not only did I learn how to create better environments for women to thrive; I, in turn, thrived with this unexpected growth in my personal development and business.

The same potential exists for you and those you lead.

So what are some of the questions you can ask yourself to help you step into this space?

CREATE ENVIRONMENTS FOR YOU AND OTHERS TO THRIVE

1. What are five ways you've organized your environment that contribute to you thriving?
2. What are five ways you've organized your environment that prevent you from thriving?
3. What are five new ways you can create opportunities for yourself to thrive?
4. Of the people you lead, who seem to be thriving the most? What environmental factors have you established that contribute to their success?
5. Of the people you lead, who seem to be struggling the most? What environmental factors have you established that are potential obstacles to their success?

DESIGNING ADDITIONAL PRINCIPLES TO SUPPORT YOUR LIFE AND WORK

The three Principles of On Purpose Leadership are your foundation for preventing drift and staying on a powerful course.

You may also find that you wish to design principles that are specific to the goals and objectives of your own life and those you lead.

I would encourage you to master these three before going too far down the path of authoring your own. Your competency in living these three principles first will naturally allow you to expand and refine other principles that are specific to your world.

For example, Ray Dalio uses hundreds of principles to govern his life and his business.

Ray Dalio is one of the top-100 wealthiest human beings alive. *CIO Magazine* called him "the Bill Gates of investing."

He is the founder, co-chairman, and co-chief investment officer of Bridgewater Associates, one of the world's largest hedge funds. As of September 2019, his net worth was a casual $18.7 billion.

Dalio attributes his radical success to organizing his entire life – investing, leadership, culture, decision making, personal growth – around a meticulous series of principles that guide his every move.[9]

In September of 2017, Dalio published his first book, *Principles*, which swiftly rocketed to a number one *New York Times* Bestseller and is endorsed on the cover by Bill Gates, Arianna Huffington, and Tony Robbins.

His philosophy is that if you make one well-informed decision upfront (defining a principle), you eliminate thousands of other potentially poor decisions in the future.

When you are ready, you may choose to do the same.

---

9 - Success as defined in the traditional sense: financial and social status. I have very little insight into the success of his relationships or his inner world of peace and/or happiness.

Here are some powerful examples of principles you can borrow or use to inspire yourself as you create your own:

"You become what you believe."
– Oprah Winfrey

"Mastering others is strength.
Mastering yourself is true power."
– Lao Tzu

"Whatever the mind of a man can
conceive and believe, it can achieve."
– Napoleon Hill

"If you don't like something,
change it. If you can't change it,
change your attitude."
– Maya Angelou

"Value the important over the urgent."
– Stephen Covey

DESIGN MORE PRINCIPLES TO SUPPORT YOUR LIFE

1. What are your top five, non-negotiable values?
2. Where do you often drift Off Purpose, and how can you design a principle to keep you on track?
3. What are your favorite quotes that you find yourself referencing most often?

IN SUMMARY

On Purpose Leaders subscribe to a defined set of principles where intentionality and integrity guide every behavior..

Principle #1: Master the Art of Leading Yourself Before Leading Others

Principle #2: Everyone Wants to Be Led

Principle #3: Create Environments Where You and Those You Lead Can Thrive

Now that you're living On Purpose, in alignment with your principles, it's time to take action.

Effective action requires a plan.

In the next chapter, we will focus on the tools at your disposal for developing sound plans.

CHAPTER 4

ON PLAN

In early 2018, Mindy O'Connor found out she was going to be a grandmother.

She was elated, feeling a fresh spark for life that had been missing for quite some time.

But with this burst of energy also came a sobering reality.

With the way she was living her life, there were no guarantees that she would be in optimal condition to see her grandchild grow up.

As a senior executive in business development for a large financial services company, Mindy had lost all semblance of a work-life balance, burning the candle at both ends with nonstop travel, indulgent client meals, and a total lapse in exercise routine.

She was the heaviest she'd ever been, and her energy levels were low.

More alarming, she felt her life was controlling her, instead of Mindy being in control of her life.

Mindy was tremendous at masking her inner discontent from the outside world because she was always so great at delivering on other people's needs.

Everyone else was more than happy to keep on receiving from Mindy. After all, they were getting what the needed.

On and on this cycle of exhaustion and ambivalence continued.

Mindy then made a life-changing decision.

On August 1st, 2018, she launched a plan for her new way of living: *The Year of Mindy*

For the next 12 months, Mindy committed to putting herself first.

When she did this, she realized it was time to move on from 20 years at one company so she could seek a culture that lived the work-life balance that she craved. Within three months, she found that new place, where she remains today.

Around that same time, she started a 30-day fitness challenge (a project) to get her health back in order.

That 30-day project kickstarted an identity shift, from "putting my needs before others is selfish" to "I best serve others when I feel 100 percent, and that means prioritizing my health and fitness."

In a period of only 4 months on her new fitness regime, Mindy "lost 19 inches from various parts of [her] body, which allowed [her] to shrink back into [her] old wardrobe."

Mindy has been inspiring many by sharing her Year of Mindy story on the stages of sales conferences, women's business groups, and national industry events.

In February 2020, she received "the best annual performance review [she'd] ever gotten in [her] professional career."

Mindy is On Purpose, living more of her life from her Greatest Energy, and her work performance is soaring as she leads others to design their own "Year of Me."

WHY YOU NEED A ONE-YEAR PLAN

Mastering the art of leading yourself won't happen overnight. It requires deep desire, commitment, and a plan of execution.

Mindy's one-year plan kickstarted a profound upgrade in every facet of her life.

Including becoming a leader who inspires and impacts others.

Your one-year plan will create a focus and clarity for how to live the next 365 days On Purpose.

The first step is to ask yourself:

?

What if the next year of your life could be the most meaningful, prosperous, and fulfilling year of your life?

- What experiences would you want to have?
- What skill sets would you want to develop?
- What relationships would you want to forge?
- What relationships would you want to leave behind?

If you keep on doing things the way you've been doing them, are you on track to live the best year of your life?

These are really big questions that you have likely not given yourself enough space or time to contemplate.

You know what it's like to drift through time: One day bleeds into the next...one week, one month, one year, one decade...even an entire lifetime.

That's how Mindy was living until the pending birth of her first grandchild snapped her out of drift and put life-changing structure around her next 12 months.

Living On Purpose won't happen by accident; you have to bring intention, constantly, in everything you do.

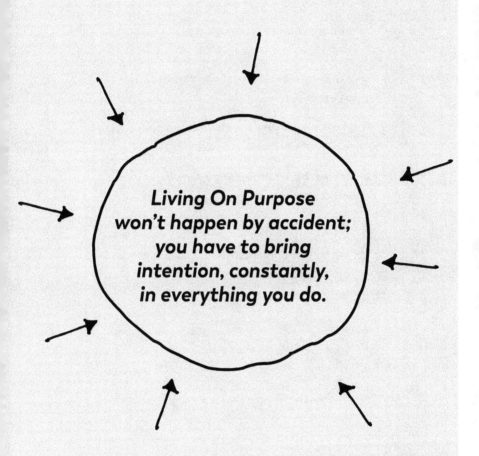

As you prepare yourself to design a plan for the next year of your life, you will want to ensure:

» Your plan is built around the things that give you your Greatest Energy.

» Your plan is aligned with and guided by the Principles of On Purpose Leadership:

1. ***Master the Art of Leading Yourself Before Leading Others.***

2. ***Everyone Wants to Be Led.***

3. ***Create Environments Where You and Those You Lead Can Thrive.***

Let's begin.

THREE STEPS TO DESIGN THE NEXT YEAR OF YOUR LIFE

I'm going to walk you through a process for planning, so you may want to read through this first and then come back and work through the action the steps.

Step #1:

Do an Inventory of Your Previous Year

As Maya Angelou says, *"How can you know where you're going if you don't know where you've been?"*

Let's first take a look at where you've been.

Review Your Memory

Write down your standout moments from the previous year.

Look for:

- » Peak experiences
- » Beginnings and endings
- » Births and deaths
- » New relationships and relationships that ended
- » Places you traveled
- » New habits you formed, old habits you broke
- » Disappointments and hardships
- » Recurring themes

Once you've done this download from your own memory, then follow the next steps.

Review Your Calendar

If you keep a calendar on Google, Outlook, or still have an old-school planner, flip through the last 12 months and amaze yourself with all of the meetings, travel, and experiences you've forgotten.

Review Your Journal

If you keep a journal, this is your time to scan or reread the entries from this past year. Look for themes and topics that you write about often; these are clues to where your energy and attention is focused.

Look for turning points and subtleties that otherwise may go overlooked.

Review Your Social Media

Scroll through your social media accounts and look at what you posted over the previous year. Look at the pictures, the places you've been, and who's in the photos with you. How do you look – happy, sad, neutral?

Read your captions and assess the tone and themes of your posts. Are you positive, negative, emotional, dry, braggy, insecure?

Make a note of everything you notice and the things you think went well and those that didn't.

In summary, here's why it's important to do a review of the last 365 days:

Get clear and present on what you want to leave behind

- Get clear and present on what you want to carry forward
- Use this reflection to design your next 365 days ahead.

Step #2:

Pick a One-Word Theme for the Year Ahead

Bryan Stacy, my good friend and co-pilot on *The Great Man Within* podcast picked his first "one-word theme" back in 2017.

His word for that year was "intentionality."

He didn't really even know what he wanted to do with intentionality upfront, but he felt like he'd been moving through life doing a lot of activities but without a lot of purpose or anything meaningful to show for it.

In 2017, when decisions came his way, instead of reflexively saying yes, he filtered it through a lens of intentionality, asking: *Does this energize me and connect me to a sense of purpose?*

That was the year Bryan took his first step on the inner

journey by coming on my Design Your Future men's retreat in April of 2017. That kickstarted a passion for inner work and a desire to devour books and podcasts on personal growth.

By early 2018, Bryan had grown so much that I asked him to start co-facilitating workshops with me here in New York City. In January of 2019 we launched the podcast. By September of 2019 he helped me co-facilitate a three-day men's retreat.

All of these significant life developments and personal growth can be traced back to the roots of Bryan's one word: intentionality.

Now it's time to choose your one-word theme.

If it's easier for you, feel free to do what Mindy did and pick a one-sentence theme: The Year of Mindy.

You'll know you have a winner when:

» You feel CLEAR on the "why" of your year ahead.

» You feel your focus is SIMPLIFIED.

» You feel ENERGIZED.

Step #3:
Take Inspired Action

My one-word theme of 2019 was "love."

So my first action was to sign up for a four-day workshop on relationship intimacy with John Wineland.

That project was a success, so I promptly committed to a nine-month intensive with John that's been some of the most meaningful personal development work I've ever done.

My one-word theme of 2020 is "community," so I launched a mastermind of 20 men – The Great Man Mastermind – who will be working together for the next 12 months on living their purpose and realizing the best versions of themselves.

This stuff works, if you work it.

As you take inspired action, ask yourself:

» What is the one action I can take right now to get me into motion?

» Am I following my Greatest Energy?

» Is this in alignment with my Principles?

» Is my plan forward clear, simple, and energizing?

Now that you've got the protocol to design the best year of your life, it's time to live The Year of You.

As you start living The Year of You, you will quickly notice how long 365 days can be. New challenges, goals, and projects will emerge that either have the potential to keep you on plan, or pull you off.

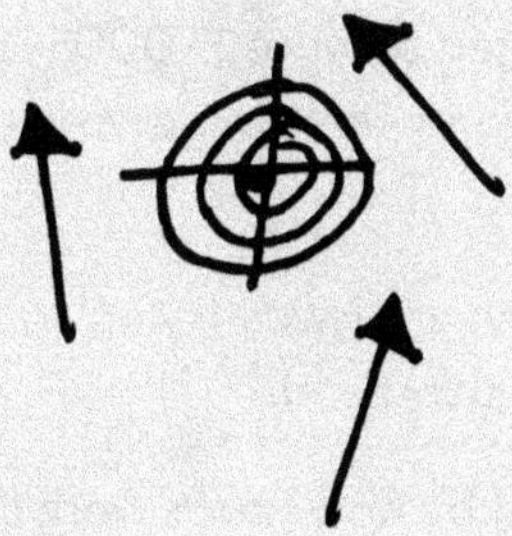

OFF PLAN (AND HOW TO FIX IT)

In 2017, when I set out to write my first book, *Design Your Future*, I did so with fervor, reckless abandon, and a complete absence of a plan.

I'd like you to picture a seven-year-old child dumping a 5,000-piece *Game of Thrones* Lego set out on the floor and snapping pieces together without even knowing whether he was building a castle or a spaceship.

That was me, writing my first book. My first attempt was a baby step above what you'd classify as "an unmitigated disaster."

The extent of my plan was that I had a cool title, some decent stories, and the drive to start typing.

Somehow, I managed to write 15,000 words – which had no logical sequence or flow, mind you – before I stalled completely.

When it came to where I was trying to take the book, I was at a complete dead end.

I was overwhelmed by how much work I'd already put in and yet was miles from the finish line.

I'd lost all energy and felt defeated.

Before I'd started writing, it all seemed so clear. I had a great idea for a book, belief in myself, and the drive to put in the work.

But when the rubber met the road during the execution phase, I was incredibly ill-equipped.

That's when I decided to hire my editor, Kelly Irving.

I proudly presented her my early progress of 15,000 words. To which she reviewed and said, "These are great! And we're going to start from scratch."

Gulp.

Kelly ushered in a plan that corrected my course immediately.

She had me fill out a book template that got me super clear on the "Why" of my book, the biggest problem standing in the way of that "Why," a simple model for "How" to overcome the problem, and "What" steps my reader needed to do to in order to achieve their "Why."

Kelly put me on a three-month writing schedule with regular check-ins to ensure progress and maintain momentum.

Suddenly, I was clear on everything I needed to do to write a book I could be proud of.

The path forward wasn't exactly easy, but the steps were simple.

Just like that, my energy to write again was back full force.

Within three months, I had written my first book.

The point?

All the inspiration in the world won't help you successfully bring that dream into reality. As the saying goes, success is 1 percent inspiration and 99 percent perspiration.

I perspired a lot on my way to 15,000 words, which Kelly eventually trashed. But what I really needed was to perspire in the right direction.

As Benjamin Franklin once said:

"By failing to prepare, you are preparing to fail."

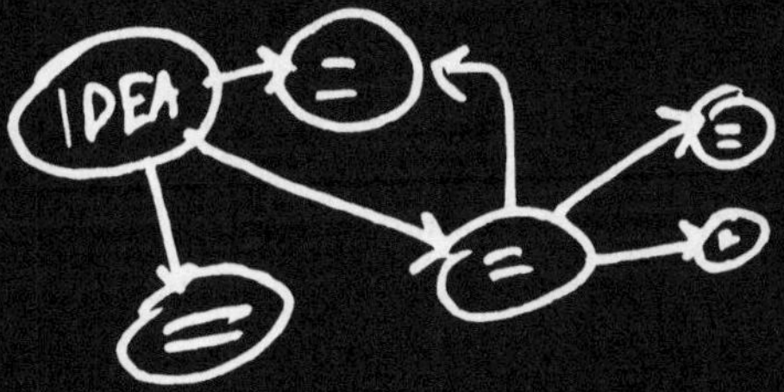

A sound plan channels all your effort into your desired payoff.

"PLAN YOUR WORK AND WORK YOUR PLAN."

I love that saying by Napoleon Hill.

Mastering the art of developing and executing sound plans is the difference between you having dreams and *living your dreams.*[10]

I know from personal experience.

Once upon a time, I took a personality assessment called the Kolbe Index.

On a scale of 1 to 10, I scored a "9" on the category of Quick Start, which meant I likely have a natural ability to innovate, improvise, and spring into action in a moment's notice. These were all true based on my life's experience.

The shadow side of being so quick to launch into action is I'd often do so without a plan.

Sometimes my reckless enthusiasm paid off. Most times I'd find myself 30, 40, 50 percent down the road

10 - Napoleon Hill often uses the term "sound plan," so this is yet another tip of my cap to the man.

on something when I'd hit a dead end, give up on what I'd started, and then beat myself up for wasting time and energy.

My big plans, hopes, and dreams remained just that.

Can you relate?

On the other end of the spectrum, I work with clients who get paralyzed in the planning phase.

They have a tendency to overthink, over worry, and attempt to solve for every variable before taking the first step. This is what Jim Carrey would call "fear disguised as practicality."

Between paralyzed and reckless, there's a happy medium called a sound plan.

When you develop a sound plan, you will stop talking about your dreams and start living them.

A sound plan does these three things:

1. **Clarifies:** You know why, how, and what you're doing.
2. **Simplifies:** It takes the complex and makes it straightforward.
3. **Energizes:** You feel driven, ready, and prepared to take inspired action from your Greatest Energy.

Let's look at each.

#1. A Sound Plan Clarifies

In my first attempt at writing *Design Your Future*, I wasn't clear on why I was writing the book in the first place:

- What was the specific problem I was trying to solve?
- How did I propose to help solve the problem?
- Who was I trying to help?

When taking on a project that requires the type of time and energetic commitment that writing a book does, you need to be damn clear on why you're doing it. Otherwise you're certain to get stopped when things get difficult (like I did).

When it comes to the people who come to me for coaching, I see no shortage of genuine desire or willingness to make change, take on big challenges or pursue dreams.

But I see very few people who are truly clear on why they want these things, how that will make them feel if they achieve it, or what they need to do to get there.

In the absence of clarity, plans fail.

A sound plan clarifies why, how, and what you're doing.

#2. A Sound Plan Simplifies

In Jocko Willink and Leif Babson's best-selling leadership book *Extreme Ownership*, they reference an underperforming sales organization.

As they interviewed the sales team, they quickly learned the salespeople were mystified by their company's sales compensation program.

When Jocko and Leif consulted the architects of the program, they soon figured out the problem: the comp plan required a PhD in astrophysics to understand.

While it was technically a work of art, it was overly engineered, wildly complicated, and none of the salespeople could understand a damn thing.

If you know anything about salespeople, you'll know if they don't understand their comp plan, they don't sell very much.

Jocko and Leif worked with the comp team to make dramatic adjustments to the plan to simplify and incentivize behaviors that benefitted both the company and the salespeople.

Sales shot up shortly thereafter.

If your plans for execution are too complex, you'll confuse yourself and the people you lead, and your well-intentioned plans will die a slow death.

A sound plan simplifies, taking the complex and making it straightforward.

#3. A Sound Plan Energizes

Losing energy is the silent assassin of your best-laid plans.

It's often a byproduct of complexity and lack of clarity. In the case of writing *Design Your Future*, I slowly started to feel my energy and desire to write the book wane until I gradually lost all motivation.

The energy dissipates so subtly and over an extended period of time that you almost end up in a place where you've forgotten why you were ever interested in the first place.

But you can also lose energy even when you have clarity and simplicity.

Why would this happen?

This happens when there's something about your plan that is Off Purpose.

For example, after the first 18 months of doing one-on-one executive coaching, I was very clear on how to create breakthroughs for my clients, and the process for doing so was straightforward.

My clients were delighted with the results of their work; they were referring me new clients, and my young business was taking off.

However, I found my energy for coaching waning, even when the results were fantastic for everyone involved.

When I checked inside to inspect this confusing feeling, I realized that my Greatest Energy came from facilitating group discussions, while one-on-ones often drained me emotionally.

In this sense, losing energy is a tremendous clue. It signals that something is out of alignment with your purpose, principles or the plan itself.

If your energy isn't dialed in at peak potential, especially when you're climbing the big mountains, your plan will fail.

A sound plan energizes so you feel ready and prepared to take inspired action from your Greatest Energy.

THREE QUESTIONS TO ASK YOURSELF PRE PLAN

1. Does this plan CLARIFY why you're doing this, what benefits it will bring, how you're doing it, by when, and who's responsible?
2. Does this plan SIMPLIFY the actions you must take for the path forward?
3. Does this plan ENERGIZE you to take timely, inspired action?

FIVE PLANNING TOOLS TO HELP

We're about to get really tactical about developing sound plans.

But hey, tactical is where execution lives.

Chances are you've dreamt up some big ideas for your one-year plan:

» Starting your own side hustle

» Getting in the best shape of your life

» Writing a book

» Speaking on 10 stages in the next year

» Meditating for 365 straight days

Those are big commitments that require a concentrated effort over an extended period of time. Remember, life will undoubtedly throw obstacles in your way and threaten to take you off plan.

That's why you need to fortify your plan upfront by leveraging a series of planning tools.

Whenever I'm about to embark upon a big mission, I always ask myself:

"What tools will give me the best chance of executing this plan?"

Here are your five tools to fortify your plans:

1. **Systems:** Repeatable processes with defined steps designed to produce an expected outcome.

2. **Projects:** A series of tasks to be completed in service of a desired outcome.

3. **Periods of Time:** A clearly defined time horizon marking a start and finish.

4. **Scorecards:** A method of tracking progress and calibrating success.

5. **Accountability:** A structure of support to ensure follow through.

Sometimes one or two of these will be enough to help me execute a plan.

Other times, I need to employ all five of these tools to successfully construct and execute a clear, simple, and energizing plan.

The point here is bringing awareness to the levers you can pull to enhance your opportunity for execution success.

#1: Systems

A system is a series of defined steps designed to produce an expected outcome that can be repeated over and over again.

Well-designed systems clarify, simplify, and energize.

Examples of systems include:

» A morning routine

» A weekly workout routine

» A repeatable process for taking notes and retaining information while reading books

#2: Projects

A project is a series of tasks to be completed in service of a desired outcome.

Projects differ from systems in the sense that they are typically unique, whereas systems are designed to be repeatable.

Sometimes a project has a clear beginning and ending (like writing a book), and other times it can be something less bound by time (like learning a language).

Examples of projects:

» Writing a book

» Learning a language

» Building a house

#3: Periods of Time

Defining a specific time horizon, marked with a clear beginning and ending, often provides the *energizing* benefit.

Have you ever finished a meeting where someone says, "I'll complete XYZ task," but fails to commit to a date of delivery?

You know that thing will drag on longer than you want.

Open-ended projects or initiatives can often drag on forever without accountability.

Example of periods of time:

» Deliverable is due by 5:00 p.m. Friday

» A 90-day, one-year, or 10-year plan

» A six-month period of service as a community leader

#4: Scorecards

A scorecard is a method of tracking progress and calibrating success.

When you're embarking upon a long-term journey, you'll often find yourself in the position of doing a lot of work long before the desired payoff will be in sight.

For example, when Jerry Seinfeld was an unknown comedian, he knew that his road to comedic mastery was going to be a long one. To bring energy and a sense of progress into his daily existence, he constructed a simple scorecard that measured one thing:

"Did I practice comedy today?"

If he did, he'd mark an X on his calendar. If he didn't, he'd leave the day blank.

As he started this practice, he soon found tremendous joy and a spark of energy in the growing chain of X's marked on his calendar.

He felt such a sense of accomplishment of his streak that his rallying cry became "don't break the chain."

We all know how that turned out for Jerry Seinfeld.

Scorecards are extremely useful tools in bringing a sense of progress and payoff into the present.

Examples of Scorecards:

» A box score in baseball
» A checklist
» A project plan with deliverables, deadlines, and due dates

#5: Accountability

Let's get one thing clear about accountability: The best type of accountability is support based, not fear based.

Somewhere along the line, accountability turned into a punishment-type energy.

We hear terms like "I need a throat to choke," which makes accountability feel like a guillotine is hanging over your neck.

When you – or the people you lead – are in a place of fear, there's no way you can operate from your Greatest Energy.

This is where you drift from your Principles and eventually end up way Off Purpose.

On Purpose accountability:

» Is administered with the energy of support, not punishment

» Holds to a high standard

» Is always tied back to being On Purpose, On Principles, and in the spirit of executing On Plan.

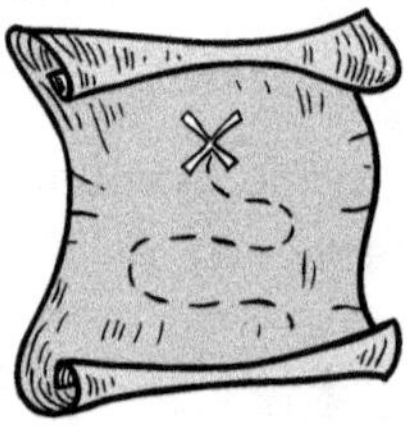

So where do you go from here?

If you haven't already started creating your one-year plan, then now is the time to go back to the beginning of this chapter and do so. First, look at the year behind you, then choose a one-word theme for the year ahead, and then it's time to take action to live that year of intentionality.

IN SUMMARY

The difference between talking about your dreams and living your dreams is your ability to master the art of being On Plan.

You now have these arrows in your On Plan quiver:

- How to design the best year of your life
- The three elements of a sound plan
- Five planning tools to ensure execution

Like I said in the beginning, release yourself from the pressure of mastering all of these at once.

Pick one arrow at a time, hold it up to your bow, and aim for the red spot in that target in front of you.

When you hit that bullseye, go for the next arrow.

CHAPTER 5

ON PRACTICES

When I first started working with Teri Kelley, a world-class financial advisor and Senior Vice President at Morgan Stanley, seemingly every minute of her life was scheduled for maximum productivity.

If she was stopped at a red light, she'd churn out emails to avoid wasting 37 seconds of potential efficiency.

Highly driven, a mother of two young boys, and the rainmaker of her business, Teri's days were stacked from start to finish. Even her personal time was intense, having competed in five IRONMAN competitions to date.

Like many high achievers, she had scheduled no time for recovery in between any of this "stuff".

On March 14 of 2019, at the age of 43, Teri had a heart attack.

Or so she thought.

Her husband called 911, and a group of six paramedics rushed to her home, lifted her onto a stretcher, and put her in the back of an ambulance.

Fortunately, it turned out to be something far less serious than a heart attack but equally bewildering: Teri had experienced a massive panic attack.

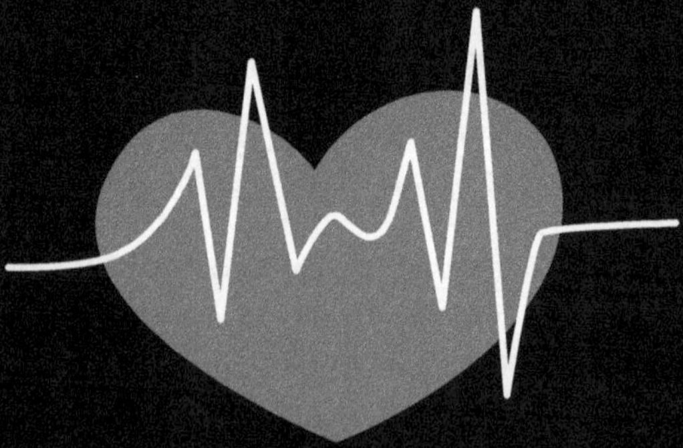

Once her cardiologist determined she hadn't had a heart attack, he asked Teri about the dynamics of her lifestyle.

Teri revealed she'd been living in a constant state of stress over a multiple-year period. She had bought-out two other advisory businesses and burned the candle at both ends trying to integrate them into her own.

Right before the panic attack, Teri finally could see the finish line in sight. The two businesses she'd bought were nearly integrated, and she'd finally hired additional support staff to help with the load.

As soon as she felt some semblance of relief, boom, the panic attack hit her.

This is more common than you would think. In the heat of battle, you can keep it all together and suppress things like fear, sleep deprivation, and the need for recovery.

But once the battle nears its end, every bit of your wellbeing that you've been overlooking comes screaming to the surface.

It's not much different than when you go on vacation and immediately get sick. Your body finally stands up for what it's been suppressing for so long.

How did Teri, someone so intelligent, talented, and hard-working end up in a place where she almost did irreparable harm to herself?

A little drift at a time.

When you're playing big games like Teri, it's easy to make little concessions like forgoing workouts and squeezing in "one more work thing" before bed, which eventually expand little by little, over time, to a full attack on your health.

There's no way you can be On Purpose while you are under a constant state of stress and anxiety.

That's why it's essential you have a *daily practice* designed to head drift off at the pass.

Teri needed to establish a daily practice that provided her space. Space for recovery. Space to breathe. Space for her own wellbeing.

The first place Teri and I targeted was creating space for a morning routine.

When I first started working with her to implement this morning routine, she resisted. With her two young children, there was no space for "Teri time," and on some level she found prioritizing her own needs to be self-indulgent.[11]

Despite her initial resistance, Teri was willing to give 10 minutes a try.

It consisted of some breathwork, a few minutes of meditation (she was a first timer), and journaling.

After a rocky start (I caught her cutting corners a few times), she stabilized and found her rhythm.[12] Her routine started to feel good and pay dividends.

When the weather turned nice, she added running to her morning routine.

What was at first an extra "to-do" in her already packed schedule, her morning routine started to provide lasting benefits – peace of mind and focus – throughout the day.

---

11 - A common theme for many women.

---

12 - I know you're reading this and smiling, Teri!

Most importantly, she felt like she was in command of her life again.

On some days she'd dedicate 30 to 60 minutes. On other days she did five minutes.

Teri will be the first to admit that she's not "perfect" with her morning routine. Some weeks involve crazy travel, sick kids, and unexpected demands that call for real-time adjustments.

She had to learn the lesson that the point of a morning routine is not to be rigid or perfect but to be flexible so it remains a consistent part of your daily practice.

Over time, the space that her morning routine provided allowed another buried desire to surface: Creating space for deep, meaningful connections with friends.

Over the past two years, Teri's friendships had taken a backseat to the demands of work. She realized she had a craving to connect with other inspiring women who could call her forward in life.

She committed to a practice of making regular space for

prioritizing relationships. Over this past year, she's carved out time with friends to take hikes, took a girl's trip to Montana, and she's even in the process of kickstarting a monthly women's group.

While there are some weeks where she finds herself enveloped in work and slipping back into the grind of things, there is one key difference: Teri now catches these slips. Her daily practice, starting with her morning routine, is always there.

But the difference now is, she catches it.

Her daily practice, starting with her morning routine, is always there.

It serves as an anchor to ensure she stays On Purpose.

WHY YOU NEED A DAILY PRACTICE

The quality of your lifetime is not determined by how you live your years.

The quality of your lifetime is determined by the quality of how you live each and every day.

I see too many leaders under-emphasizing the importance of living each day with intentionality, instead racing around, drinking from the firehose in a manic effort to "get it all done."

This is a terrible long-term strategy, the consequences of which we saw with Teri.

Each day you live swept up in the frenzy of to-dos and putting out fires, you are literally practicing to continue living that way into the future.

If you want to master the art of leading yourself and live a life On Purpose, you need to practice differently.

You need to have a daily practice that supports living this way.

Your daily practice is your ritualized series of behaviors that keep you On Purpose and in your Greatest Energy.

Your practice sharpens your sword.

Athletes don't just play games, they practice.

Actors don't just show up on stage, they practice.

Monks don't just become monks; they have a practice.

You need to be in practice, every single day.

You need to operate from three foundations to ensure you are On Practice:

1. **Optimize the Bookends of Your Day:**
   Develop morning and evening routines.

2. **Create Your Own Practices:**
   Sharpen your sword.

3. **Implement Team Practices:**
   Sharpen your team's sword.

Let's start with what I've found to be the single biggest point of leverage in elevating your daily performance: optimizing your morning and evening routine.

OPTIMIZE THE BOOKENDS OF YOUR DAY

Bookend #1: Your Morning Routine

Throughout the better part of my twenties, my morning routine looked a lot like this:

1. Wake up
2. Eat Frosted Flakes
3. Watch *SportsCenter*
4. Poop
5. Shower
6. Go to the train station

The only true intention of my morning routine was to get me out the door and to the office on time. In that respect, it sufficed.

But as my jobs became bigger and my life became more complex, I found myself increasingly more anxious and scattered throughout the days, and exhausted when I came home at night.

It didn't feel like my work was suffering, but my mental, physical, and emotional wellbeing sure were.

Can you relate?

Your morning routine is responsible for the quality of all the waking hours that follow.

But very few of us have intentionally designed our morning routines.

Chances are, your morning routine happens to you.

Most people's morning routine looks like some version of:

1. Turn off alarm clock
2. Look at cell phone
3. Flood mind with news and other incoming noise
4. Race around the house getting ready
5. Rush out the door
6. Get to office and then think about the day ahead

How'd I do?

The process efficiency legend Edwards Deming once pointed out that the first 15 percent of a process (your morning) dictates 85 percent of the outcome (the 16, 17, 18 hours that follow).

Is your present-day morning routine (first 15 percent) intentionally designed to support what you want for the remaining 85 percent?

If you're like most people, you could use a tune up.

A well-designed morning routine allows you to access your Greatest Energy first thing in the morning.

Get in Your Greatest Energy

Before you choose what you'll be doing during your morning routine and deciding how long to dedicate, you first want to decide what you want to feel throughout the day.

I have different answers for this question depending on which type of day I have in front of me:

1. **Standard day:** Typical days where I wake up at home
2. **Non-standard day:** Running retreats, keynote speeches, travel days

For example, on my standard days, I want to feel:

» Energized

» Clear minded

» Clear on the #1 thing I need to do to make the day a win

On non-standard days, like when I'm giving a keynote speech, my desired feelings are slightly different: Energized

» Clear minded
» Service mindset (focused on audience impact vs. me looking good)

Knowing the feeling I want to carry with me for the next 16, 17, 18 waking hours, I can then reverse engineer:

» What I need to fuel my body (food and exercise)
» What I need to fuel my mind (focus, planning)
» What I need to fuel my soul (Purpose and spirituality)

Now it's your turn.

1. On your standard days, write down three things you want to feel as you go throughout your day. Do the same thing for your non-standard days.
2. Now write down two or three things you can do in the morning to support you feeling that way.

Your morning routine should provide stability and consistency to your life, but you also don't want to be overly rigid with being 100-percent perfect every single day. Some days are spent in travel.

Some days are more demanding than others.

Be willing to adapt.

Your morning routine should adjust to the ebbs and flows of your dynamic lifestyle.

Remember, your morning routine can begin with as little as 10 minutes, like Teri. It has to be something you can reasonably execute five days a week, for at least three weeks.

I'd rather you start smaller and allow your time to expand as you experience the benefits, versus over-dedicating too much time that cannot be sustained in the long run.

Once you get 15 wins over a 21-day period, you'll inevitably feel the benefits. At this point, most of my clients will end up dedicating more time to their morning routine because of how much payoff they're experiencing.

You might even end up like Jeff Bezos, who is a self-proclaimed "putterer" around the house in the mornings. He intentionally doesn't get to work on anything before 10:00 a.m., which he claims gives his mind space to breathe, power up, and think clearly.

I've personally experimented with all sorts of timeframes – 10 minutes, 45 minutes, two hours, and everything in between.

However, it's important to note that I'm single and without children, so I have a lot of flexibility in how I design my mornings. This structure may not be possible for you with others in the house demanding your attention. Don't compare yourself to me. Make it achievable for you.

Here's seven ideas that I've personally used, and continue to use, for myself and with my clients that create a daily practice that supports On Purpose living.

SEVEN MORNING PRACTICES TO TRY

1. **No phone**

   Most people will wake up and dive right into their phone, getting lost in tasks and setting themselves up for a reactive, small-minded day. Instead, dedicate the first 15 to 60 minutes of your day to setting up or executing on the most important things you're committed to for that day.

2. **Breathwork**

   If you're like me, it takes me a while to shake off the cobwebs in the morning. At least, it used to be that way for me before I started doing a five-minute morning breathwork practice.

   There's a variety of "activation" breathwork exercises you can Google. I prefer Wim Hof - which quickly gets your blood flowing and oxygen to circulating to the most crucial parts of your body. My clients have been amazed at how refreshing this feels and how quickly they're able to get into motion in the morning now.

3. **Meditation**

   As Victor Frankl is credited with saying, "Between stimulus and response there is a space. In that space is our power to choose our response. In our response lies our growth and our freedom." Once your day gets going, it's nonstop stimulus and response from top to bottom. Meditation is your way of slowing down the game, creating that pause, and empowering yourself to make new choices that facilitate growth and freedom.

4. **Journaling**

   Think of journaling as a way to get to know the most awesome person in the world: You. We spend so much of our time focused externally that we're wildly disconnected from what's going on inside. If you find it difficult to journal, don't be alarmed, it was for me too. It's simply a sign that you haven't built the muscle around going inwards. Once you get into the habit, you'll be amazed at how much goes on inside of you. This will allow you to refine your awareness around where you place your inner attention.

5. **Exercise/Walking**

   In the book *Spark: The Revolutionary New Science of Exercise and the Brain* by John J. Ratey, powerful scientific research shows that exercise produces something called brain-derived neurotrophic factor, which is like Miracle-Gro for the brain. In layman's terms, exercise not only gets your blood pumping, but it primes your brain for optimal thinking, retention, and comprehension.

6. **Creating Something**

   We are consumption machines. We consume news, social media, television, music, podcasts, the list goes on. So **Create** something instead. Before I fill my mind with external noise, I love tapping in internally and coming up with content ideas, new business ventures, or making a 60-second video on my phone to send to someone who's impacted my life.

7. **Spiritual Practice**

   I love reading spiritual texts first thing in the morning because it grounds me in the bigger picture and prevents me from getting caught up in the small stuff. Some of my clients have reported feeling deeply inspired and peaceful by reconnecting with scripture or prayer in the morning, which they've carried with them throughout the day.

   And, if you want to dive even deeper, Hal Elrod's *Miracle Morning* is an entire book dedicated to designing your "miracle morning" routine.

2 Bookend #2: Your Evening Routine

It's important to understand that the quality of your morning routine is heavily impacted by the quality of your evening routine.

How you spend your last hour of the day will directly affect how you feel in the first hour of the next day.

But if you're anything like me, evenings can often finish sloppily.

After navigating a full day of demands on your time, attention, and energy, it's highly likely your tank is near empty and your capacity for willpower and discipline is at its lowest points.

That's why many evenings look like:

» Finish work you didn't to during the day

» Dinner

» Glass of wine

» Put kids to sleep

» More work

» Second glass of wine

» Late night sugary sweet treat

» Collapse into bed with phone/tablet/tv

» Binge watch too many episodes

» Disappear down news/social media rabbit hole

» Pass out

Any of this feeling a bit too real for you?

Don't fear; I was there once too.

If you're passing out at night, stuffing your belly, and clogging up your mind with gibberish shortly before lights out, you're already sabotaging your ability to wake up On Purpose.

Not only that, but you're decimating the quality of sleep you're getting. More and more research has shown that the quality of sleep you get (deep sleep, REM sleep) is every bit as important, if not more so, than the quantity of sleep you get.

Eating too closely before bed, flooding your body with sugars during sleep, and exposing yourself to blue light are all sure-fire ways to downgrade the quality of your sleep.

You're actively setting yourself up to be tired, mentally foggy, and less than 100 percent when you wake up the next day.

Hence, your morning routine actually starts the evening before.

Because your tank will be empty at the end of the day, with the least amount of discipline and willpower at your disposal, it's essential you have a well-established ritual to support optimal behavior.

Rituals become habits.

Habits don't require willpower or discipline.

So, when you're fatigued, you allow your evening-routine programming to run on autopilot.

Here are seven tell-tale signs to check for.

SEVEN WAYS YOUR EVENING ROUTINE IS SABOTAGING YOU

1. You "pass out" instead of consciously falling to sleep.
2. You don't have a regular 90-minute window when you go to sleep.
3. You don't plan your next day's top priorities.
4. You don't do a reflection of wins/losses/insights of the day you just had.
5. You use your cell phone as your alarm clock.
6. You eat too much and/or eat too close to falling asleep.
7. You get into bed with your phone.

Design Your Evening Routine

There are three stages to the evening routine:

1. Hone your 90-minute "go-to-bed window."
2. List your "top three" for tomorrow.
3. Design your wind-down ritual.

Let's work through each of them.

1. Hone Your 90-Minute "Go-to-Bed Window"

I recommend establishing a 90-minute sleep window:

» This is your target window for lights out (e.g., my window is 10:00 p.m. to 11:30 p.m.).

» Aim to be lights out during this window, five nights a week.

This window gives you structure during your evenings.

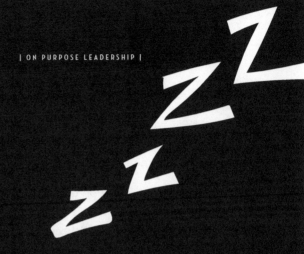

It helps you to determine whether you start that next piece of work (or watch that next episode of *Succession*) or not.

I'm bullish on the sleep window because it's been the single most important contributor to my energy levels the next day.

According to most sleep experts, one of the most critical habits you can develop for high quality sleep is to get to bed at a regular time.

This is where most of us wave the "but that's not practical based on my lifestyle" flag. After all, you're not a child who can establish a regular 9:00 p.m. bedtime. I imagine your life is a bit more complicated than that.

That's why establishing a 90-minute window – like 10:00 p.m. to 11:30 p.m. – gives you flexibility. If you aim to hit this window five nights a week, you'll be in good shape.

I measure my sleep stats on a daily basis using the Oura Ring, which at the time of this writing is considered to be the most accurate wearable device on the market.

On the nights where I get to bed in my 90-minute window, I average noticeably more deep sleep (an increase of 20 to 25 percent), which is critical for healing, brain function, and muscle repair.

I've even found that when I go to bed during my 90-minute window, I can get less sleep with higher quality than if I were to go to bed outside my window and sleep in longer. For example:

» **Better Quality Sleep for Me:** Going to bed at 10:30 p.m. and waking at 5:30 a.m. (7 hours)

» **Worse Quality Sleep for Me:** Going to bed at midnight and waking at 8:00 a.m. (8 hours)

YOUR TURN TO ACT

1. Identify your 90-minute sleep window.
2. Determine how many nights per week you'll fall asleep in that window.
3. Create a scorecard or mark a calendar to identify the days you executed.

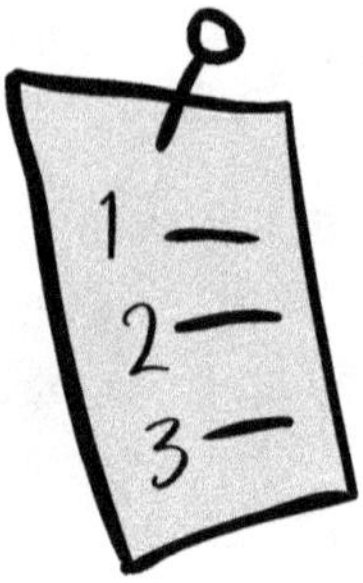

2. List Your Top Three for Tomorrow

Your last piece of "work" for the day is to plan your focus for tomorrow.

Being On Purpose means getting clear on "the top three things" to do before noon the next day that would make the day a win.

If you were to complete these three things before noon, your day would be a success.

This practice keeps you focused on what's mission critical and helps you avoid drifting into your emails, texts, social media, and everything else that's Off Purpose.

Sometimes it can be just one thing. For example, my one thing for today is to finish editing this chapter. I estimated three to four hours of work, which meant I cleared my morning schedule and haven't even touched my phone yet today.

It's not important whether it's one thing or three things; what's important is that you're clear on your top priority for the next day and that you've created space to tackle it first.

Remember to keep this list in a visible place.

Out of sight often means out of mind. If you choose to keep your list in your phone, just know you may be sabotaging yourself with potential distractions such as texts, emails, and social media.

I write my top three list down on a note card and place it on my kitchen counter so I can bypass my phone and ensure it's the first thing I see in the morning when I wake up.

YOUR TURN TO ACT

1. Identify the part of your evening routine where you will list your Top Three for the next day.
2. Identify the visible place you will post your Top Three.
3. Clear any obstacles in your way of executing on your Top Three.

3. Design Your Wind Down Ritual

Your last 15 to 30 minutes should be your ritual for kickstarting your physical, mental, and emotional wind-down process.

This means avoiding any unnecessary stimuli (I'm looking at you, cell phone) that will derail your process of winding down.

My last 30 minutes usually looks like:

- » Turn off phone and leave in kitchen.
- » Put on blue light blocking glasses.
- » Take 3mg of melatonin (some nights, to assist in wind-down process).
- » Brush teeth and wash face.
- » Read fiction to clear my mind.

As I instituted this ritual, I found that over time, as soon as shut my phone down for the night, I had this Pavlovian response where I could feel my body physically switch to wind-down mode.

With an On Purpose evening routine, your sloppy evenings will gave way to an intentional system shut down.

Your mornings will start stronger.

For the next 16, 17, and 18 waking hours, you'll be unstoppable.

YOUR TURN TO ACT

1. Identify three to five things that contribute to your settling down in the evening.[13]

2. Identify how long you need to wind down and synchronize that process so you fall asleep in your 90-minute window.

3. Plan how you will intentionally fall asleep vs. pass out.

13 - Preferably non-substance related.

CREATE YOUR OWN PRACTICES

We dove deep into the morning and evening routines because those are two practices that will immediately interrupt drift and allow you to feel in greater command of your life.

Once you experience the power of being On Practice, you'll likely want to institute other practices that contribute to your optimal performance as an On Purpose Leader.

Here are some examples of other powerful practices to inspire your thinking:

BILL GATES
Practice: Think Week

While he was the big boss of Microsoft, Bill Gates would escape by himself to an undisclosed location in the Pacific Northwest for a practice he called Think Week.

For an entire week, twice a year, Bill would go completely off the grid so he could quiet the noise of the external world and have space to contemplate the future of Microsoft (and eventually, humanity).

During this week, he'd read up to 18 hours a day.

He would often come home with trajectory-changing insights and clarity for the future of Microsoft. An example of this is when Microsoft launched Internet Explorer back in 1995.

JULIA CAMERON
Practice: Morning Pages

Julia Cameron is an acclaimed author, artist, poet, and mentor to creatives. Her most famous book, *The Artist's Way*, has sold over four million copies and is renowned for its practical practices on how to ignite creativity and innovation in your life.

The most popular practice is what she calls Morning Pages: a first-thing-in-the-morning ritual of stream-of-consciousness writing download into a journal.

Authors Tim Ferriss and Elizabeth Gilbert both attribute creative breakthroughs to the Morning Pages process.

No matter what comes to your mind, you write it. No

evaluation or critique. This is simply done to empty the clutter of your mind. You're not even allowed to read it afterwards.

As it turns out, the same gunk clutters up your mind on a daily basis, prohibiting new thought to surface. Once you clear the gunk through Morning Pages, there's an outlet for new ideas, creativity, and inspiration to arise.

PAUL BRUNSON

Practice: Focused Morning Time with His Wife

Paul Brunson is a serial entrepreneur who routinely juggles multiple businesses and carries the honor of having had Oprah as a mentor.

I interviewed Paul for *The Great Man Within* podcast and learned how he and his wife resuscitated their marriage off of life support.

Every morning, after they drop their two young kids off at school, they share their love of coffee together for 30 to 60 minutes. They exclusively focus on their relationship, banning any discussion around kid stuff or the mundane logistics of life.

If your lifestyle doesn't permit that, get creative with how it would.

For example, Ryan, one of our brothers in The Great Man Mastermind has an annual year-end practice with his wife called "Sex and Strategy." Every December, they leave the kids with the in-laws and take a week-long retreat somewhere exotic and spend 50 percent of their time vacationing, and the other 50 percent investing in developing their relationship and intimate lives.

GEORGIA O'KEEFE

Practice: A Gentle Morning Routine

Georgia O'Keefe was an American artist and national treasure.

In the book *Daily Rituals: How Artists Work* by Mason Curry, she describes her morning practice for accessing her Greatest Energy:

> I like to get up when the dawn comes. The dogs start talking to me and I like to make a fire and maybe some tea and then sit in bed and

> watch the sun come up. The morning is the best time, there are no people around. My pleasant disposition likes the world with nobody in it.

O'Keefe would allow herself a leisurely 30-minute walk and a breakfast around 7:00 a.m. Her mind clear and her well-being tank full, she would step into her painting studio primed for creation.

JOHN WINELAND

Practice: No Striving Time

John Wineland is a teacher of Masculine Leadership, guiding men to lead more consciously and powerfully at work, home, and in the bedroom.

During my interview with John on *The Great Man Within* podcast episode entitled "The Art of Masculine Leadership," John shared that men get trapped in the hamster wheel of "constantly striving."

Meaning, our default gear is achievement, productivity, and performance. It's exhausting.

The way most men balance this exhaustion is through numbing and escape: emotional eating, drinking too much, binging on TV, etc.

These unconscious escapes don't rejuvenate the mind, body, and soul.

Instead, John encourages his students to build in 30 minutes of "no striving time" per day – which you can do all at once or break out into segments.

Examples include:

» Meditating

» Staring at the ocean

» Walking aimlessly

» Playing

» Listening to music

I cannot emphasize enough the need to master your morning and evening routines first, as they will only help amplify the power of implementing other practices you design.

Now go forth and design some of your own!

FOUR QUESTIONS TO KICKSTART THE PRACTICE PROCESS

1. What are your gateways to accessing your Greatest Energy?
2. How can you build these gateways into your daily life?
3. How can you create extended practices - like Bill Gates' Think Week - around your Greatest Energy?
4. How can you invite the most important people in your life - like Paul Brunson does with his wife - into your practice?

IMPLEMENT TEAM PRACTICES

Once you've discovered the power of having regular practices for yourself, you'll want to introduce and implement practices with your team.

Here are three practices I've helped leaders establish with their business teams, romantic partners, children, and communities.

#1: Begin in Gratitude

Practice Intention: Set the tone of the meeting from a place of appreciation, and squeeze extra juice out of life's best gifts and blessings.

My mentor of six years in Strategic Coach, Lee Brower, taught me this practice, which he used every Monday morning with his staff meetings.

He called it "Go BIG" (begin in gratitude).

I've used this with teams to forge bonds that run deeper than professional, surface-level relationships.

This is the type of practice that inspires going the extra mile and giving discretionary effort.

Process:

» At the beginning of a meeting, give each person 30 to 60 seconds to express something personal (and/or professional) that they are grateful for.

» Ask them to express WHAT or WHO they are grateful for.

» Ask them to express the WHY they are grateful for this.

Coaching Tip:

Most people will need coaching to drill deeper into WHY they are grateful.

For example, you'll typically hear something like:

"I'm grateful for the health of my children."

But when you help guide someone to the WHY, you'll hear something like:

"I'm grateful for my son's health because when he was born with all his health complications, we didn't know if he was going to make it. Now he's in kindergarten, happy and healthy as can be with a bunch of friends. It's been such a relief for my wife and I, and we've been able to refocus on the strength of our marriage. I can feel tears welling up in my eyes as I speak about it."

#2: Physical and Emotional Check-In

Practice Intention: Building emotional fluency, connecting with what's happening inside of us right here and now, and communicating it with others.

Process: Each person has 30 to 90 seconds to "check in" physically and emotionally.

» Participant closes his/her eyes to go inward.

» Start with: "This is Dominick, checking in."

- Physically I feel _____, _____, ______.
- Emotionally I feel ______, ______, _____.
- End with: "I'm here and I'm in."

A physical check-in could sound like:

> *"Physically, I feel warm. I feel the gum in my mouth and my feet on the floor. I'm tired. There's pain in my left knee and an ache in my forehead. My chest is relaxed, and my stomach is settled."*

An emotional check-in could sound like:

> *"Emotionally, I feel confused. I don't feel much right now. OK, now I feel anxious in my stomach. There's a tightness in my chest that feels like nervousness. Now it's gone. I feel a lightness spreading across my forehead and I feel joy. I feel excitement about seeing my children tonight."*

I've used this with corporate financial services teams. There's always awkwardness at first, but once the practice is established, teams end up loving it.

That's because you'll hear things surface that wouldn't otherwise, like, "Emotionally, I'm feeling confused because I don't know what my role is in this meeting and we don't have an agenda."

This is a practice that takes what's buried – or most important – and brings it to the surface.

If there's an important meeting that's 60 minutes or longer, dedicating five minutes to this upfront has shown to get teams on the same page much faster.

Use With:

» Your primary work team

» Your romantic partner

» Your children

#3: Withholds

Practice Intention: Enhance transparency, resolve conflict, and elevate communication.

Definition of Withhold: A withhold is anything that's standing in the way of you being present with the person or group in front of you.

By expressing it, you allow what's in the way to be spoken and cleared so you can connect more fully.

Sounds Like:

> *"Jerry, I have a withhold. I've been waiting for that write-up you promised me yesterday, and I still haven't gotten it, which is effecting my ability to get my work done on time...and I'm frustrated."*

> *"Team, I have a withhold. I said I was going to follow up on the project and I haven't. I'm embarrassed and feel like I've let you down."*

"Team, I have a withhold. I've been dealing with some family issues at home that have my mind preoccupied right now. I'm doing my best to let that go, so if I seem scattered, it's not because I don't think this meeting is important. If you see me drift, please call me back in."

Process:

» **Withholder says:** "James, I have a withhold," or "Group, I have a withhold."

» **Listener(s) says:** "Would you like to share?"

» **Withholder says:** "Yes..." and then shares withhold.

» **Listener(s) says:** "Thank you for sharing."

That's it.

This is not meant to spur debate or discussion. It's simply meant as a way to clear whatever was in the way of the withholder being present.

Sometimes the withhold is directed at someone in the room. That person gets *one* opportunity to respond, if he or she chooses, using the same formula as above.

And then it's done.

The agreement in this practice is that when the withhold is directed at you, that it's your responsibility to go inwards and reflect on that, to find truth in what was shared, to integrate it and move forward.

There's two ways to establish this practice:

1. **Dedicated time for withholds:** In my men's group, we dedicate three minutes to this practice before our meetings start. We set a timer, let it run, and wait for someone to speak up. Sometimes there are no withholds. Sometimes, when there are many withholds, we go a minute or two over.

2. **Allow withholds as they arise:** Give your teams permission to say at any time, "Group, I have a withhold." We also welcome this in our men's group meeting, so you can encourage both.

IN SUMMARY

A well-designed practice:

- Keeps you On Purpose.
- Provides instant access to your Greatest Energy.
- Heads off drift at the pass.

By optimizing the bookends of your day with your morning and evening routines, the quality of the 16, 17, or 18 waking hours in between will continue to improve.

By designing your own personal practices to support your unique lifestyle, you will master the art of leading yourself.

By implementing regular practices with your team(s), you will master the art of leading others.

Congratulations!

You've officially navigated through
the four tenets of the On Purpose Protocol:

MY PURPOSE
Leaves This World a Better Place Than I Found It

MY PRINCIPLES
Show Me the Way

MY PLAN
Makes Victory Inevitable

MY PRACTICE
Sharpens My Sword

The blueprint for On Purpose Leadership
has been laid out before you.

It is yours for the taking,
if your desire is strong enough.

AS NAPOLEON HILL SAYS:

"Desire is the starting point of all achievement, not a hope, not a wish, but a keen pulsating desire which transcends everything."

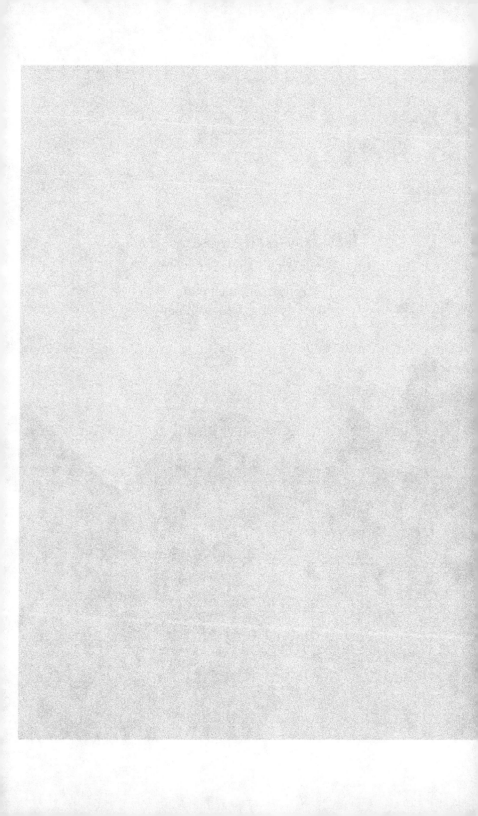

A LIFE LIVED ON PURPOSE

I'm pretty sure no one else remembers my finest professional moment.

It was 2015, and I was still working in the corporate world, running a sales team for Prudential Retirement.

Tim Sanders, best-selling author of the book *Love is the Killer* App, was on stage delivering the keynote speech at our national sales conference.

He introduced the concept of a "Love Cat," a silly name he uses to describe an invaluable type of coworker. A "Love Cat" is a person who is generous with the sharing of his knowledge and his network and genuinely supports and contributes to the success of others.

While the name itself generated its fair share of eye-rolls, we all agreed that we dig those types of colleagues.

During his speech, he asked our audience to think about who the Love Cats were among us. He said we wouldn't have to think too hard; they'd be fairly obvious.

Then he asked us to pull out our phones and text the names of our Love Cats to a number he posted on the big stage screen.

Soon, on the big screen, a list of the names started popping up.

I remember feeling a surge of pride when I saw my name pop up for the first time.

Just as quickly, I made sure to swallow any public expression of emotion because I already knew the rest of the sales guys would be busting my balls about being a *"Love Cat."*[14]

Sanders then took the dozen or so names and listed them vertically on screen, numbering us 1 through 12.

He asked us to take out our phones again.

---

14 - Why not Boss Dog, or Big Daddy, or the term branded on Samuel L. Jackson's *Pulp Fiction* wallet?

"Text the number of the ONE person who you think is most deserving of the Love Cat status in your organization. The results will populate real time on this screen. You get ONE vote."[15]

The sea of 200 of us in the audience pulled out our phones and started submitting our votes.

"Let's see that first refresh!"

The big screen went blank for a moment...and when the names reappeared, a bar chart of results popped up onto the screen.

The bar next to my name went off the screen.

No one else was close.

As the results continued to refresh, I maintained my lead.

I won handily.

---

15 - Side note: I'm a keynote speaker. In my experience, any time you rely on the slightest bit of technology, I'm talking the slightest bit, you're rolling the dice. I bow down to this man's courage for the fact that his presentation hinged on this text-to-screen exercise.

This whole thing had happened so fast, going from sitting passively in an audience of 200 people one minute to being recognized by your peers as "the most generous and genuine person" in the business a moment later.

I felt tears well up in my eyes as they called me to up the stage to be recognized while trying my damndest not to let those tears roll down my face.

If I had to do it again, I'd let the tears fall.

To me, there was no bigger honor than knowing I'd shown up, every day, as a man who contributed to the work and lives of others, and it was recognized and appreciated by everyone around me.

Out of my 15 beautiful years with Prudential, amidst all the meaningful work, the promotions, closing the big deals...

...THIS was my proudest moment.

For me, the Love Cat experience was a moment of arrival.

I'd been living On Purpose for five years – quite imperfectly, mind you – but with a relentless commitment to mastering the art of leading myself and finding purpose in the here and now. When the entire organization of my colleagues publicly recognized me as the man I'd been working so diligently to become, it was one of the most meaningful moments of my life.

I also realized this stuff works.

My twenties were a blur of sameness and drift. Sure, I can point out some pivotal experiences and proud moments like at any point in my life. But overall my twenties felt like a flickering light bulb that wasn't fully screwed in.

This last decade of my life, from my thirties to early forties, feels like a high-powered flood light. These past 10 years have felt like an entire lifetime, in the absolute best of ways.

If you were to tell the Dominick of 2010 that the Dominick of 2020 would living a life where I'd be:

» Running my own business, making a real impact on people's lives

» Working with clients I genuinely love

» Living a lifestyle designed around my Greatest Energy

» Speaking on stages around the world

» Feeling freedom from a 20-year addiction

» Running a mastermind for men doing inner work

» Being a leader in bridging the gender gaps in the workplace

» Co-hosting an acclaimed podcast with an audience around the world

- Being surrounded by the most inspiring people on a daily basis
- Authoring a book, twice (and I ain't done yet!)
- Having a community of followers who trust me and are living their lives On Purpose...

I would've given up everything in my possession to trade for the life I have now.

Fortunately, I didn't need to trade anything.

These were all natural evolutions of living a life On Purpose.

And it's only been a decade.

So ask yourself this:

What would happen if you lived the next 30 days On Purpose?

What about the next 30 years?

Imagine the energy, power, and command you'd feel in your life.

What would happen if you played the game of organizing your life so you could eventually spend 80 to 100 percent of your time in your Greatest Energy?

What would happen if you surrounded yourself with a community of people who called out the Highest Version of you?

What would happen if you lived your life guided by your Principles, executing on your Plan, and supported by your daily Practices?

What would happen if you lived the next year like that?

What about the next decade?

What about the rest of your life?

Can you imagine the vitality you would feel in your daily living and the impact you'd have on the world around you?

The greatest leaders of all time – our heroes like Napoleon Hill, Barack Obama, Oprah Winfrey, Viktor Frankl, and Ruth Bader Ginsburg – have lived their lives On Purpose.

It's why we admire them and follow them even when they've physically left this earth.

It doesn't matter if you're 22 or 72; it's never too late to start living On Purpose.

Your path to On Purpose Leadership always begins with understanding:

1. You must master the art of leading yourself before you can effectively lead others.

2. You must see your present-day work as a portal to your Purpose, right here and now, in order for you to lead from your highest potential.

The beauty is you don't need to be perfect about any of this.

All you need to get started is a desire and a commitment to walking the On Purpose path.

I know, because I've been on this path for the last decade, and it's led to the most meaningful moments of my life.

So now I ask you:

Are you ready to live a life On Purpose?

Are you ready to find meaning and purpose in the present while building a lifetime of memorable moments?

You have the protocol.

All you need is the desire and commitment to begin.

I'll see you on the path.

Dominick

LET'S CONNECT

Hey, it means the world to me that you've read this far. Even if you skipped to this page, we're still friends. If you've been inspired to move from reading to taking action, here are ways we can work together.

KEYNOTE SPEAKING

If you need an inspiring, relevant, and energizing leadership message for your next event, let's talk.

CUSTOM TEAM RETREATS

I help teams accelerate personal leadership, install systems of accountability, and optimize communication in as little as 48 to 72 hours. I will work with you to design an offsite retreat that will get you and your team On Purpose, fast.

Dominick@DominickQ.com
DominickQ.com

CPSIA information can be obtained
at www.ICGtesting.com
Printed in the USA
JSHW020339190820
7318JS00010B/1

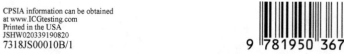